Y0-BQV-919

THE LIFE OF
THOMAS HARDY

Thomas Hardy, 1923. From the painting by Augustus John, A.R.A. The
original now hangs in the Fitzwilliam
Museum, Cambridge.

THE LIFE OF
THOMAS HARDY

BY
ERNEST BRENNECKE, Jr.

NEW YORK
GREENBERG, PUBLISHER, INC.
1925

CONTENTS

[v]

APOLOGY

*I*N putting together this biographical account it has been my hope to place at the disposal of Thomas Hardy's readers some material which may add a certain amount of richness to those profound emotional experiences which are created by a sympathetic perusal of his imaginative works. I have purposed to accomplish this by means of description—of the man personally, with his simple human likes and hates; of his interesting ancestry; of his surroundings; of his experiences. Among the last I have included purely intellectual, purely artistic events and influences, as well as superficial, physical happenings.

This will indicate that the following pages include some account—even some comparative study—of Hardy's books; possibly to the annoyance of those who seek in a "life" a complete divorcement from criticism, and a concentration on the sensational possibilities of the subject's career.

There is, therefore, little "spice," and perhaps too little "story," in this book. For this lack there are several contributory causes: There was very little "story" in Hardy's life. Very meagre information, regarding even that little, is possessed even by Hardy's intimates. Hardy is at this moment still alive; to tell too much, even if one could, would be indelicate, impertinent.

Hardy was a man whose chief occupation was writing.

Apology

He simply sat down and wrote. Other things which he did are unimportant, except in so far as they affected his writings. As far as his masterpiece, *The Dynasts,* is concerned, for instance, it is far more important to realize what Æschylus wrote in the Sixth Century B. C. than it is to know whether Hardy dipped his pen in black ink or lavender ink. Still, I admit that if I had discovered him writing, let us say, with a quill on pink paper, I would have retailed the observation here with great unction.

To read any author without prejudice is impossible, even for the dispassionately scientific literary chemists in the graduate schools of our universities. I have therefore not hesitated to exhibit mine. I have already shown my strong preference for Hardy's poetry. Other examples of bias will be noticed. Many readers will disagree with me here and there. But to anticipate such disagreements would be to emasculate a largely personal record, such as this.

E. B.

New York, December, 1924

THE LIFE OF
THOMAS HARDY

CHAPTER I

Wessex Twilight (November, 1923)

*I*T is difficult to think of Thomas Hardy without thinking of a definitely circumscribed portion of the English countryside. And yet, when reading his novels, lyrics and dramas, one cannot help noting how universally they apply to all that is most intense in human life, how vividly they image the tragedy of human existence everywhere on our little grey planet.

Like the Athenian dramatists who found in their tiny Mediterranean peninsula a cosmic mirror wherein the whole panorama of what is richest, direst, best, worst, deepest, most colorful in the minds and actions of humanity might be discovered and artistically presented, Hardy has found in the southwestern corner of his Island all the ingredients for a complete literary picture of his time— and, in many senses, of all times.

This, in itself, is not remarkable.

What is remarkable is that Hardy, while making his discovery, has in his creative work achieved such an epic sweep, has so masterfully welded together observation,

[1]

passion and form, that he has become perhaps the outstanding literary figure of his time. Few people will now quarrel with this assertion as an extravagance.

One significant indication of its validity is the truth of the converse of our first observation, namely, that the Hardy-country has colored Hardy's work. For it is equally true that Hardy's work has indelibly colored his country, for all succeeding times and peoples. He has made a new thing of the district. He has not merely changed its name from Dorsetshire to "Wessex"; he has changed its very character, even for its inhabitants. He has made it known to many who would never have been aware of its existence otherwise. Finally, he has made it the medium by which the whole subjective world of his readers has been transfigured.

Parallelisms between Hardy and the Greeks have already been pointed out many times. Here is a new one: Agamemnon is more real today than Alcibiades; mythical Ilium more real than political Corinth. In the same way, Casterbridge and Henchard are already more real to us than Dorchester and its Mayor, whoever he may happen to be.

A "Life of Thomas Hardy," in order to fulfill its function of explaining how the man and his influence are what they are, must find facts to account, among others, for these two things: first, for Hardy's strange effect on the country; second, for the sway exerted over the world of letters by this man-made realm.

It will be necessary, then, to realize and to present Hardy in his true setting, to transcribe accurately the impression that he produces personally, to add to this an

Wessex Twilight (November, 1923)

imaginative immersion into the quality of the land of "Wessex," finally to show how the combination and interaction of these atmospheres has affected the mental world of men.

Thus a little picture must precede our ordered chronological explanation: a picture of a mind suffusing a geographical district, recreating it and driving it out into many communities by means of the instruments of literary art.

We begin, therefore, with such a picture, by way of prologue to the proper biographical history.

*   *

*

The train has rumbled past Wimborne, Poole, Wareham. A glass of heavy port at the Dorchester station takes the chill out of the dismal November journey. Now a brisk cut eastward, damp fields rolling up from below you, a dull aluminum sky pressing down from above, over fences and stiles, up the Wareham Road, and into the shadowy, rustling grove at "Max Gate." You stand under a little portico and knock. A shaggy, untidy ball bounds around the corner, knocks itself against your knees, barking unreasonably. A female voice from within:

"Wessie! Wessie! Are you misbehaving again!"

At length you are admitted, your impedimenta disposed of. Mrs. Hardy, dark, small, preoccupied: "The dog is a nuisance . . . Still unused to callers . . . Loves attention . . . Mr. Hardy will be glad to see you. He will not write autographs. He has had some unfortunate ex-

[3]

periences with interviewers. Still, there are many visitors. Miss Amy Lowell has been here, and Mr. Clement Shorter, and Mr. Dudley Field Malone, an American—who is Mr. Malone?''

Wessie tries so furiously to eat wood out of the fireplace that he is at length led away, struggling, whining.

The room is dim, furnished plainly, low-ceiled. There is a portrait of Shelley on the wall.

Meanwhile Hardy has come down. He is small, somewhat stooped; grave and kindly in manner. Deep-set brooding eyes look out from a framework of wrinkled parchment. They look out dispassionately; yet they dominate. He wears a fuzzy sweater beneath a thick grey-green suit.

''People at last seem to be discovering the curious charms of this part of the country. Even on dull days like this, I daresay, one can love it.''

His voice is even, vibrant, slightly high-pitched, with a strange questioning inflection to each cadence. It makes everything he chooses to say seem somehow tentative, unfinal.

''Granville Barker and his wife are thinking of settling around here. The lovely dignity of the countryside leaves its photograph on the people, you know. I've become convinced that climate really makes character. I'm sure your terrible, harsh West Virginia mountain country is really responsible for the overwhelming multiplied tragedy which you call your 'poor white' population. America is a tragic country; its tragedy is reflected in the countenances and manners of even the visitors who pass through England. But we get only vague inklings of the basis of

Wessex Twilight (November, 1923)

it, such as the periodic outcropping of your Negro problems and other racial difficulties. I am too old ever to
fathom this; I can only feel it vaguely, like a faint echo
of a cataclysm on another star.

"I can't even always fathom quite the charm of the
ancient church musicians about here. They serenaded me
with some old tunes the other evening. That sort of thing
carries me back to the fifties—even to the forties. I'm old
enough to remember the gaudy Napoleonic military uniforms, with their long flapping tails. Their fascination
has been a lasting thing. Dashing uniforms give me
pleasant sensations."

Slightly inconsecutive is the Hardy discourse, but
quietly dynamic. Sometimes the gears of memory actually slip for a moment. Minor characters in certain of
the Wessex novels, for instance, have become quite submerged.

About other things there are flashes which brilliantly,
electrically illuminate the fading past. At the mention
of Swinburne, "I loved Atalanta," he confesses, simply.
"I used to walk from my lodgings near Hyde Park to the
draughting office every morning, and never without a copy
of the first edition of the *Poems and Ballads* sticking out
of my pocket. It was a borrowed copy . . . If I'd only
bought it at the time, it would be worth many guineas
today.

"Tennyson and Browning both lived near me. For two
years I read only poetry—no prose, except the newsprints
—a curious obsession! Well, I still believe poetry to be
the very essence of literature . . . No editors even
touched my verse for many years. Oh, yes, I sent much of

it out; it invariably came back. And I destroyed a good deal of it.''

Luncheon is announced and served by trim maids. There is cider—''Sweet cyder is a great thing,''—one remembers the swinging lyric of life-love. The conversation veers.

''You have some mighty promising poets in America. Who is Louis Untermeyer? I'm very fond of his verse. It's keen. But he's not a rebel, is he? I don't fancy revolutionaries. I never moved in revolutionary circles, even in the sixties and seventies when Darwin set London aflame. Blomfield, my architectural master, was a clergyman's son, you see. I liked the artists best. I liked the quiet galleries.

''We've just been reading Dreiser's *Genius*. What does one think of it?''

Mrs. Hardy, serving the custard and plum-pie: ''We think it ought to be suppressed—really!''

Hardy holds up a finger: ''Not because it's immoral. It may not be. But because there's no excuse for a writer's deliberate abandonment of any kind of form. One prefers—expects—some sort of structure, not a mere heap of bricks, no matter how excitingly red they may be. . . .

''Yes—perhaps I shouldn't carp. The clergy burned poor *Jude* in a public bonfire. . . .''

Mrs. Hardy has retired as the whiskey-and-soda begins to be sipped. Wessie romps in as the door swings to. Hardy carefully slices up bits of cheese and feeds them to the poodle.

''Worst of all, people have often tried to identify me

Wessex Twilight (November, 1923)

with Jude. That's an impertinence, don't you think? *Jude,* anyway, is the least autobiographical of all my novels. Where they seem most autobiographical, they are least so. This is generally true of imaginative writing. I remember being struck at one time by a description of an execution in France, in one of Arnold Bennett's novels. It seemed to strike so clearly the note of truth and reality. Later I discovered that Bennett had never even seen a guillotine.

"Young Springrove, in *Desperate Remedies,* was actually drawn from life, it is true—but not from my life. It was a youth I once knew quite well. He's now dead, poor fellow. . . ."

You find yourself back in the drawing-room. Hardy continues chatting amiably. He takes down from his shelves a heavy volume, turns the pages abstractedly. You venture to admire a Hardy portrait, facing the Shelley on the opposite wall.

"We like that one," says Mrs. Hardy, detached, half-dreamily. "Another used to hang there. We tired of it. One day Mr. Hardy tore it up."

Mr. Hardy allows himself a twitch of a smile, although he continues to look elsewhere.

"Now here," he observes, proffering the book, "is a fellow who has written about me with some enthusiasm. Only he has gone to my novels instead of to *Who's Who* for his facts. He's been impertinent in spots, you see. We've corrected him; I've penciled some notes in his margins. Perhaps you'd care to look over them, if you're interested."

A quaint preoccupation, this.

The Life of Thomas Hardy

The notes have been set down with a fine, careful pencil. The characters are beautifully formed. You look as though you'd like to copy the remarks. Mrs. Hardy fetches you a sheaf of paper. Here are a few of the items you scratch off:

The birthplace of T. H. was not a humble cottage; it was (and is) a low, but rambling and spacious house with a paddock and (till lately) large stablings.

This is impertinent.

Primary school 8th to 10th year only—see *Who's Who*.

He knew the dialect as a boy, but was not permitted to speak it—it was not spoken in his mother's house, but only when necessary to the cottagers, and by his father to his workmen, some 6 or 12.

First to London & the suburbs, then from place to place—Somerset & the Rhine, etc., then Sturminster-Newton, then London several years, then Wimborne. 3 or 4 months every year to London for nearly 30 years, in flats & houses rented for the season.

Hardy stands and watches you silently as you turn the leaves. He has lit a cigarette, holds it in steady fingers, puffs meditatively. He opens a glass china cupboard, takes out a small painted porcelain model of a vine-covered, thatch-roofed house. A curious bit. Whatever can it be used for? Then he tells you that it's a reproduction in miniature of his birthplace. You can get one, he says, for one-and-six at the curio shop in East High Street, just above St. Peter's. Hardy feels strongly

[8]

about that house. He was not born in a Lincoln log-cabin.

The talk shifts around, somehow, to the teaching of English writing. Can writing be taught? Hardy thinks so. He wants to know why they don't teach the writing of verse. It's the best method of learning how to handle words and sentences, he says, even if one's final object is the writing of clear and vivid prose.

"I never wanted to write prose novels at all. I was forced to manufacture my novels; circumstances compelled me to turn them out. All the time I composed verse. I wrote verse for years, long before I thought of writing prose. Lyrical activity was essential for my existence—and *The Dynasts* was crying for materialization, crying to be born, for many years. I wrote it because I had to, because of orders from within. It really wanted to come out in one burst, like a lyric—but the flesh is weak; I had to do it in three parts. . . .

"Max Beerbohm's burlesque of *The Dynasts* in his *Christmas Garland* gave me plenty of amusement. It's the cheerfulest parody on anything of mine that I've ever seen. I like Max. . . .

"Was it really difficult to get the earlier editions of *The Dynasts* in America? I'd heard something of the sort. If that ever happens again, do write me and I'll see what can be done about it. There's now a convenient pocket edition. I've only one copy, or I'd let you take it with you . . . It can be read on a railway journey. . . ."

We are outside in the garden. Max Gate is covered with ivy leaves. It is a solid, unbeautiful, four-square house, but it squats there with a quaint dignity.

The Life of Thomas Hardy

"I had some German prisoners working for me out here in the garden during the early days of the war. Nice fellows. The villagers used to gather around late in the day and talk to them, although it wasn't officially permitted. They got on together very well. The Germans happened to speak some particular variety of Saxon dialect; our people spoke their own country-tongue, a direct descendant of King Alfred's Anglo-Saxon, as William Barnes pointed out.

"Now a remarkable thing happened. The Wessex Old English and this Low German were so similar that there was almost perfect understanding between the two groups.

"When I noticed this, I went inside and composed a sonnet. It was printed in the newspapers shortly afterwards, and created something of a storm. Patriotic people didn't like it. But the facts of philology and the real bonds between people of the same race are stronger than a temporary war-fever. I daresay few people remember the sonnet now, or consider it an amazing thing if they do."

You happen to remember it. It is called *The Pity Of It*:

> I walked in loamy Wessex lanes, afar
> From rail-track and from highway, and I heard
> In field and farmstead many an ancient word
> Of local lineage like "Thu bist," "Er war,"
>
> "Ich woll," "Er sholl," and by-talk similar,
> Even as they speak who in this month's moon gird
> At England's very loins, thereunto spurred
> By gangs whose glory threats and slaughters are.

Wessex Twilight (November, 1923)

Then seemed a Heart crying, "Whosoever they be
At root and bottom of this, who flung this flame
Between kin folk kin tongued even as are we,

"Sinister, ugly, lurid, be their fame;
May their familiars grow to shun their name,
And their brood perish everlastingly."

What an Argive curse is here! What an ardent vengeance and pity! What an ardent meliorist is this aged man!

This thought colors your next utterances.

"No," says the poet. "I am not."

Mrs. Hardy takes her leave. She has vanished to look after her brood of chickens.

"I am not interested in Mrs. Hardy's chickens. And really, you must not ever call me 'ardent' about anything. I am not. I am as indifferent as I find it possible to be. I wish you success, however. Good-day."

    *   *

  *

Amazing, curious visit! A physically feeble man, more than eighty-three years old. But keen-witted, with a strange, slippery logic to cover an enigmatic personality. A memory but fitfully illuminated, and in unexpected places. A touch of common simplicity, a strain of common nobility. An unflinching grip on reality, and a sentiment that trembles at the touch of things.

An aura surrounds Max Gate, a twilight aura that suffuses the district and its people. One feels it even outside Wessex, of course, even before one treads the Wes-

sex soil. One feels it in New York and in London and
Paris; one hears its quiverings in scraps of talk, in the
strange wistful twist with which people force themselves,
quasi-incredulously, to speak of the material reality of
the Wessex poet. "Wessex" lives: the novels, the lyrics,
The Dynasts, The Queen of Cornwall, but that Wessex
domain is the creation of a mere man who sat down to put
mere words to paper. This man has now achieved a
spiritual tyranny over what could be, before his time,
only the after-life of the old Kingdom of Alfred the
Great. Wessex the idea, the Wessex of the mind, that is
to say the real Wessex, is now Thomas Hardy's own. To
one who has surrendered to the experience of this idea,
the physical southwest English county known as Dorsetshire has passed out of existence.

*   *

*

Well, you walk back into Dorchester. (No one will mistake you if you call it Casterbridge). You pause to look
into the window of a stationery shop. The usual photographic post cards are displayed for sale. But they don't
show "real" places at all. They are, for the most part,
captioned and sold as illustrations to the Hardy novels
and poems. Few sets for Dorchester, but many sets for
The Mayor of Casterbridge and *The Woodlanders.* The
aura is not merely "literary." Not even the natives consider their own countryside as something real. Their
familiar places have little to do with ponderable matter;
the "real" people who now go to and fro in them are
only phantoms. These places are real only in so far as

Hardy attending a rehearsal of *The Queen of Cornwall* at the Corn Exchange, Dorchester, in the summer of 1923.

Wessex Twilight (November, 1923)

they are the places where Clym Yeobright and Tess Durbeyfield rejoiced a little and suffered much. Thomas Hardy is a wizard who has enchanted the land, turned it into something which has no longer an objective existence. Its imaginative, subjective reality is so much stronger.

All this is of course just a mood, and perhaps a deceptive one. All the same, it's there; and being felt, it's real. And in the years to come, you may reflect, Wessex might indeed partake of a magic comparable in quality to that enjoyed by Stratford-on-Avon. It has already drained away some of the glamor of the Lakes.

Just see how you react to that drove of sheep trotting across the fair grounds, followed by a shaggy dog and a shepherd with his tall crook. He's not just a shepherd. He's Gabriel Oak. The Dorchester fair grounds are not just fair grounds. They are the place where Henchard sold his wife.

There are children, released from school, playing in a field. Black birds soar over their heads, flutter down and settle on the meadows. The birds are rooks. Where is the boy Jude with his clacker, to scare them away for Farmer Troutham?—and to be so terribly attacked, both by the brutal farmer and by still more brutal *Weltschmerz?*

Here are Maumbry Rings, the grassy Roman amphitheatre, surrounded by gnarled oaks, symbolic of the relentless tread of Fate. Here Michael Henchard kept tryst with his Susan, and here you, as well as Henchard (as the villagers tell you) may still, on occasion, glimpse the shades of Vespasian's legions at dusk.

The Life of Thomas Hardy

Near by is the London and Southwestern railway station; it is half-real. It links Wessex with the hinterland: Southampton and London. Standing without humor in a barren lot, it represents the antenna, the tentacle of scientific civilization, piercing the land of high romance. You think of the disheartening "progress" pictured in *The Well Beloved.*

You wander down the street again. The name hoarded above a draper's shop catches your eye. It is "Henry Knight." Instantly you are looking into Elfride's blue eyes. They are anxious, terror-stricken. Knight is hanging, clinging to the sheer face of the ghastly towering Cliff Without A Name. Wind and rain lash him grimly, bent on destroying him. He can hold out but a little longer. The eyes of a fossil in the rock survey him malignantly. . . .

It was one of the early crustaceans called Trilobites. Separated by millions of years in their lives, Knight and this underling seemed to have met in their death . . .

Time closed up like a fan before him . . .

Pitiless nature had then two voices . . .

The sea would have been a neutral blue, had happier auspices attended the gazer; it was now no otherwise than distinctly black to his vision. That narrow white border was foam, he knew well; but its boisterous tosses were so distant as to appear a pulsation only, and its plashing was barely audible. A white border to a black sea—his funeral pall and its edging. . . .

That adventure took place on the rugged coast, not many miles from this street. Doesn't it smack more strongly of reality than these woolens and linens in orderly array at the draper's?

Wessex Twilight (November, 1923)

You've reached the center of the town. Here is St. Peter's Church. A "grizzled church," built over the site of the Roman temple here at "Durnovaria"—a "grizzled church whose massive square tower rises unbroken into the darkening sky," a Perpendicular sanctuary, just as it was in the days of King John.

Outside is the statue of William Barnes, Rector of Winterbourne, the ghostly father of Hardy the poet and philologer—"an aged clergyman, quaintly attired in caped cloak, knee breeches and buckled shoes with a leather satchel slung over his shoulders and a stout stick in his hand." The inscription:

ZOO NOW I HOPE HIS KINDLY FEACE
IS GONE TO FIND A BETTER PLEACE;
BUT STILL WI' VO'K A-LEFT BEHIND
HE'LL ALWAYS BE A-KEPT IN MIND

Within the church is the Hardy Chapel, housing two cold stone effigies, reclining mailed warriors, cross-legged knights with belt, spurs, sword, shield, helmet, all of heroic proportions. Their arms are no longer visible on their shields. Time has worn away the paint from the massive granite.

A step down the street is the Dorset County Museum. Relics of many races and civilizations in the large hall inside: a Roman tiled pavement set in the floor, flint axeheads from the Stone Age. British, Danish and Saxon weapons, a map showing the location of many and various mounds. But you don't think of the Battle of Brunanburh, nor of the fleeing King and the spider's web,

nor of the legend of the burnt griddle-cakes. You think
of *The Moth Signal* on Egdon Heath:

> Then grinned the ancient Briton
> From the tumulus treed with pine:
> "So, hearts are thwartly smitten
> In these days as in mine!"

In a case under a glass cover rests a bound manuscript,
held open by rubber bands. The letters are inked with
care. You read:

CHAPTER XXIX

At this hour Lucetta was bounding along the road to Port-
Breedy just as Elizabeth had announced. That she had chosen
for her afternoon walk the road along which she had returned
to Casterbridge three hours earlier in a carriage was curious—
if anything should be called curious in concatenations of phenomena wherein each is known to have its accounting cause.

Darkness has fallen by the time you emerge into the
cold air. You are stopping at the King's Arms Hotel.
Its "spacious bow window" still "projects into the
street over the main portico," just as it did when Donald
Farfrae, the caroling Scotsman, inquired for "a respectable hotel more moderate than this."

You hurry to your room. You have ordered a fire to be
lighted, and find your quarters swimming in smoke. You
open the window. Both smoke and heat fly out. But that
doesn't matter. You descend, dine, and join the crowd
heading for the Corn Exchange. Hardy's "first real
play" goes on the boards tonight. He has entrusted his
Famous Tragedy of the Queen of Cornwall to the Hardy

Wessex Twilight (November, 1923)

Players, humble Dorset mummers. The local doctor will be Tristram, a pretty little shop-assistant will put on the robes and chaplet of Iseult of the White Hands. In the "cast" are also a greengrocer, a solicitor's clerk, a saddler, a master-brewer.

Inside the old Exchange is the audience, simple country people for the most part, seated under the oak ceiling, flanked by green-painted Gothic arches—the very scene of the Casterbridge Mayor's spectacular downfall. A local musical band, the Frampton Family Orchestra (Framptons have been mayors of the town), scrapes away on fiddles and viols, discoursing old country tunes and lively dances, for all the world like the antique Mellstock Choir. Humble folk all, here, except for a few well-fed squires whose motors are parked outside, and a sprinkling of dinner-jacketed London critics.

A microphone dangles from the ceiling in front, ready to spread the atmosphere of the evening across all England through the etheric pulsations of the British Broadcasting Company. The critics for the two-penny papers, the photographers, the microphone, seem, in a sense, to be intruders, just as you did, perhaps, when you visited the old hangman's cottage, when you trod the narrow winding lanes that brought you to the shallow Froom River and the one-time haunts of the furmity-woman.

Mrs. Hardy has come in, but not Hardy himself.

All your reflections are interrupted when the Frampton musicians suddenly silence their fiddling. The lights are switched off—on, and off again, with the customary indecision of an amateur first-night stage electrician. A projection-machine hisses and sputters fitfully in the

[17]

rear, a wavering circle of eerie green light at last finds the center of the curtain and rests there. The curtain parts, a bearded figure in a brown shroud appears in the shadows of the aperture. It begins to speak, in stiff, declamatory fashion. . . .

"There's old Tilley!" cries a woman.

But old Tilley becomes Hardy's Merlin in a moment, with his words,

> We come, at your persuasive call,
> To raise up, in this modern hall
> A tragedy of dire duress
> That vexed the land of Lyonesse. . . .

Now the "muffled shades of dead old Cornish men and women" chanting, in dragged monotone, the choral induction, as they advance and take up their stations before the proscenium. Then, as the lights disclose an exact replica of Hardy's own design for the interior of Tintagel Castle, appear the characters in the most pathetic episode in the great Arthurian legend, best beloved theme of every English poet. Again the story of Queen Iseult and her white-handed namesake, of King Mark, of Sir Tristram, child of Fate.

Your feeling is Greek. It was thus that Sophocles presented to an audience of his countrymen his own re-working of their great legendary inheritances. Here is Hardy's tragic *epos*.

The play opens in this manner, lives for three quarters of an hour, closes again like a flower, the chanters receding as they advanced, Merlin once more appearing, reciting the brief epilogue, and vanishing.

Wessex Twilight (November, 1923)

And what of you, with this impression freshly added to those you brought along with you? Well—the critics who immediately disappear Londonwards, back to the fashionable oriental glitter of Flecker's *Hassan* (only the faithful Clement Shorter remains for a second performance), will not be slow to point out, rightly, that here was given no great sweep of emotion such as a reading of *The Dynasts* gives, no thrill like the melodramatic thrill of *The Return of the Native,* or of *Tess,* or of *Jude.*

Superficial explanations of this are of course not lacking. You have learned to expect the superhuman from Hardy. And here was an amateur performance, no better, no more skilful than the usual, apart from the merits of the tragedy itself. The mind of the audience has been continually distracted by the creaking and the groaning of the stage-machinery: the audible promptings, the ill-fitting costumes with unsightly bumps on tighted male knees, the mumbled delivery of the lines, the total lack of fire and passion, the unintelligibility of the chorus's declamations, the stiff and unreal attitudes and gestures, the bad imitations of "acting." Here was neither the charming naïveté of the Irish Players, nor the practiced, polished emotion of the great metropolitan actors.

Yet you soon find compensations. If the mummers had only "mummed" the piece, and not tried to "produce" it after the manner of the late Sir Herbert Beerbohm Tree! That they were admirably fitted and experienced for "mumming" they immediately proceed to demonstrate in the two delicious old bits which follow. They are in their element: *O Jan! O Jan! O Jan!* It proves to be a variation on *The Keys to Heaven,* written

[19]

down by Hardy as he remembered it played in his father's spacious house when he himself was a four-year-old—in 1844. Astounding memory!

It is a delightful little musical folk-piece. The fashionable young gentleman cannot win the fashionable young lady's love. He appeals to Jan, the old rustic, for advice. Jan, in each succeeding stanza, advises his "measter" to offer higher inducements: a "fine silken gown," the wealth of London City, the keys of Canterbury, and finally the keys to his heart, whereupon he is accepted by the haughty fair. Between verses the three execute a beautifully grotesque dance, a "set-to" and a "hey," to the sprightly tune of *Nancy's Fancy*.

Finally, the ancient traditional play of St. George, a folk-diversion, almost a ritual, with its roots far back in the Middle Ages. The version here given is slightly more elaborate than the one which Hardy introduced so dramatically in *The Return of the Native*. Here the Dorset mummers, in their true costumes, bedizened with knots and rosettes of ribbons, panoplied with wooden swords and ridiculously inappropriate trappings, are on really familiar ground. Old Father Christmas (the Prologue), the Dragon (who supplies most of the slapstick comedy with his tail, carefully carried in his hand), the luscious Daughter of the Queen of Egypt, the four valiant British saints, Captain Slasher, the Doctor (who brings all the fallen to life with his pills), and the rest, combine in merriment to set forth a work of popular art as true as it is hilarious and entertaining.

* *

*

Iseult, Tristram and King Mark—a scene
from *The Queen of Cornwall,* as produced by the Hardy Players, November,
1923.

Wessex Twilight (November, 1923)

The performance is over. Mrs. Hardy has asked you to meet the players upstairs. Upstairs you go.

It is the large council-room. A broad, flat oak table runs down the center. Tonight it is covered with plates of sandwiches and with tea dishes. On the walls are brass plates engraved with the names of Mayors for hundreds of years back. You find yourself looking vainly for Henchard's among them. But they are all unfamiliar, until you strike T. H. Tilley's.

Tilley himself, still wearing Merlin's cloak, has come up the stairs, followed by nearly all the other players. The place is soon teeming with munching mummers, a jolly, hungry company. Tilley tells you of the past achievements of the Hardy Players. He is their General Manager. Every year they present dialect scenes out of the Wessex novels. Last year it was *Desperate Remedies*.

"My word!" gasps Tilley, "we *were* flattered when the old man gave us a real play of his—even though it wasn't quite in our line. . . . Yes, he'd drop in occasionally at our rehearsals. We'd never see him come in, though. We'd just suddenly notice him sitting 'way back somewhere in the shadows, slumped into a chair. When we'd go over to him to find out if he had any suggestions to make, why, he'd wave us off before we got near him. 'No—no—no,' he'd say. 'Just leave me alone. And don't let me disturb you. No—no— Please go right ahead. No—no, I just want to watch.' And then he'd slip out as quietly as he'd come in. Oh, he's a fine old fellow.

"There were great doings when the Prince of Wales

visited him a couple of months ago. Everybody has been wondering what those two talked about at that time. Nobody knows. But now, I could tell you a story or two —only he doesn't like us to talk about him. But anyway, maybe, after all, I might tell you—"

Tilley never tells you, because a shy young player edges in here, nervously fumbling a typewritten paper. He delivers his message in one short breath:

"I've written a poem."

He produces a fountain pen, carefully unscrews the cap, writes on his manuscript.

"Will you read it, keep it, maybe? It's about Hardy. Here's a copy. I've signed it for you."

You read:

THE WONDROUS BARD OF WESSEX

Dedicated with all respect to Mrs.
Thomas Hardy by a Hardy Player

High on the edge of Egdon Heath,
Where Sunbeams play and mists do wreath,
In thatched-roofed Cot that nestled there
Far from the Madding Crowd and glare
    The destined Bard was born.

And as a child from day to day,
He knew sweet scents of Flowers and Hay,
Whether in Cot or neath the Sky,
His waking soul was ever nigh,
    To Nature—Lessons learning.

The sprites of Woodland, Vale and Heath,
Oft flitted round like fluttering leaf,

Wessex Twilight (November, 1923)

And to the Boy with keen intent
Their message whispered—Thou art sent
    To be our Trumpet Major.

Their plaint was ever-that of them
No hand with Artist's brush, or Pen,
Had truly told of rural ways,
Sweet Spring delights or glorious days
    Neath Greenwood Tree in Summer.

Neither of Woods whose colours bold
In Autumn tints—or Winter's cold,
Which only they could understand,
Was but Dame Nature's curbing hand
    Not futile, Desperate Remedy.

He passed from Youth to Man's estate,
When Childhood dreams at last took shape,
And from the storeroom of his mind
Came forth those tales of Wessex king,
    Which make him Well beloved.

His Wondrous views of Nature's maze—
Inspired words—make beauteous Lays,
And all who scan his pages through
Can visualise the Scenes he drew,
    Of Brackened Heath and Vale.

Proud Dynasts striving Power to hold,
Or Woodlanders of Simpler mould,
Created he on Nature's plan,
And gave to them for Fiction's span,
    Moods—varied as the Seasons.

A troubled way of Storm and Stress,
Eustacia's life and that of Tess,
    [23]

The Life of Thomas Hardy

Whilst Fancy-Maid of Mellstock fame,
Resembles time of Sun and Rain,
   Twixt sowing and the Sickle.

Like broken mound on Barrowed Ridge,
Was Henchard, Mayor of Casterbridge,
For each within held Secret old;
Till Chance ordained it should be told,
   The hidden past revealing.

Hath old age dimmed! nay, now we see
The Master's hand in Tragedy,
  For Shades of Cornwall—stern and grim—
From out the past, have prompted him
   To pen Queen Iseult's story.

A tragic theme—fate haunted Lovers,
Find death beneath Tintagel's towers,
An Epic Poem the world will praise—
And pray the Bard anon will raise
   Sweet Lay—with Happy ending.

A. C. Cox.

Dorchester,
15—11—23.

You must read it charitably. Having done so, you are granted fresh insight into the processes by which Max Gate disseminates its tragic influence. Its seeds bear fruit even on stony ground. Imperfect fruit, yes. But illuminating, even by reason of its imperfection.

*   *

*

Back at the King's Arms, you toast your toes before the fire. The sitting-room is fairly cosy. The white-haired representative of a London conservative daily newspaper is there before you.

"It's good to be in a village with a warm blacksmith's forge at the heart of it," he remarks, oracularly. "I'm glad I got my critique off this afternoon . . . Clement Shorter wants to offer consolation in advance to Hardy on the rough handling he expects our papers to give the play—fancy that! As for me, well, I don't think Hardy's verses have any chewne to speak of—no chewne at all, really. Browning is often out of chewne, you know, but Hardy—no chewne, no chewne at all!"

With this echo of the literary standards of George Moore ringing through your brain, you retire to your unwarmed sheets, cursing the cold, cursing Ebury Street. . . .

You are out early the next morning. It has become colder, piercingly cold, but quite clear. You walk briskly southward along the straight hard coaching road, the old Bath-and-Bristol highway. Your train doesn't leave for a few hours; you contentedly leave the town behind.

In thirty-five minutes you look across the country to your right. There is a huge mound, almost a mountain, shutting out a great portion of the sky. You walk on. Presently a by-road turns off the highway towards the west; you follow it down a vale, passing a miniature edition of St. Peter's Church. Then over and under a few stiles. Before you is now a steeply ascending path. A post bears a weather-beaten sign:

CAUTION: ANY PERSON FOUND REMOVING RELICS, SKELETONS, STONES, POTTERY,

TILES, OR OTHER MATERIAL FROM THIS
EARTHWORK, OR CUTTING UP THE GROUND,
WILL BE PROSECUTED AS THE LAW DIRECTS.

Above you, then, is Mai Dun, popularly called
"Maiden Castle," the prehistoric British fortress,
unique in that Hardy has treated it objectively, but has
never introduced it into his transfigured Wessex. It
needs no transfiguration. The ceremonial of deification
would be wasted on a divinity.

You are tired after you have scaled the three separate
earthwork rings at the summit. An eager, biting wind
lashes you persistently. You feel the icy polar breaths
that once stung the hapless Tess on the uplands over
there. You brace yourself against them; you stand on
the edge and look out towards the north, for miles and
miles. It is a brilliant prospect.

Still, it is a dim twilight-panorama by the time your
mind has assimilated it. It is not your breathless weari-
ness that makes it seem twilit. It is the accumulation of
impressions and thoughts that have been bubbling in
your consciousness for four-and-twenty hours: the fermentation of a dominating, tyrannical mood.

A single, humble human intelligence, detached, aloof,
penetrating, pitying, has sent forth in certain printed
pages an ectoplasmic radiation that has permeated the
Kingdom you see. This transfigured Kingdom provides
vicarious tragedy, in the Greek sense of the word, for all
who find a dearth of tragedy in their lives. This miracle
happens wherever books are read on earth.

Twilight settles over it all, over the Wessex Kingdom
and over the whole spiritually enriched world, as the last

Wessex Twilight (November, 1923)

days of the great poet drift slowly into the living nothingness of the past.

Hardy the man, meanwhile, sitting back there in Max Gate, off the Wareham Road, remains unconcerned, reflective, withdrawn; darkness assailing his memory as he feeds Wessie with bits of cheese. He loves his Wessex and his verse. He admits it. Or more exactly, he is frankly interested in them both.

But he is not ardent—about anything. Why should he be? The Immanent Will Itself is unmindful, unconscious. Hardy has said it himself, many times: "Nothing that men do . . . matters much."

*   *

*

It is all a kind of miracle, this mood and this picture, this man's weird effect on a section of rich country, and on us. The core of the mystery can never be properly exposed. One can only, as time goes on, collect, assemble, digest, look at what we call "facts," and try to distill from them something like a story, something like a character-sketch. Succeeding years will bring many such trials.

Here follows one, written directly under the spell of the twilight—faulty and incomplete for that reason, but perhaps also worth more than nothing, for the same reason.

CHAPTER II

Origins (1360-1772)

*I*T was around the year 1360 that two young Norman gentlemen, brothers, of the landed family Le Hardi or Le Hardy, gathered together their portable effects and sailed across the twenty-four-mile strait that separates the Island of Jersey from the French coast. What force it was that impelled them to leave their lovely Normandy and to migrate to the lonely Channel Isle, only forty-five square miles in area, it is difficult to determine at this date. Behind them in the Duchy they left some property and possessions, which were subsequently lost to their descendants by reason of their steady allegiance to the English crown in the wars and tumults which followed. One would like to think that they were enticed away from their inherited wealth and power by the poetic lure of the cliff-skirted birthplace of the mediæval romancer Wace, that they were drawn irresistibly by the glitter of the Arthurian Legend. But one will never know.

The French branch of their family, at any rate, continued to flourish without them. Two centuries later the poetry in the Hardy blood seems to have flowered forth in Paris, when one Alexandre Hardy, author of six hundred plays, won the unofficial title of "Father of French Tragi-comedy." Contemporary of Richelieu and

Shakespeare, he became the first self-appointed educator of the Gallic taste. He presented evidence of an ambitious literary outlook in his *Les Chastes et Loyales Amours de Théagène et Cariclée,* a tragi-comedy in no less than eight "days" or dramatic poems—an entertaining precursor of *The Dynasts,* in its magnitude, at least.

To return to Jersey. Of the two immigrant Le Hardys, only one managed to make his mark in the world —if having one's name preserved in historical records can properly be called making one's mark. This was Clement Le Hardy. He had married a sister of one Sir William Lalague, or Lulazin, who brought him a dowry of "a corn rent of one quarter." He retained his ancestral Norman coat of arms, and founded the central line of Jersey Hardys, which still flourishes today. He was made a magistrate, a *Jurat,* of the island, in 1381.

There ensues a gap of over a century, during which little is known of the Hardys, except that the office of island *Jurat* was passed down from father to son without interruption. But it was a stirring century for Jersey. The island had long ago sworn allegiance to King John of England. The French, however, naturally considered it their own: was it not a good hundred miles removed from Portland Bill? In 1404 they descended in force upon the disputed territory, but were promptly repulsed. Then came the Wars of the Roses. Queen Margaret, consort of Henry VI, in order to win for the King the support of the Seneschal of Normandy, the Comte de Maulevrier, promised him the islands as his reward. Maulevrier accordingly attacked Jersey and captured Mont Orgueil, the ancient fortress, built on the site of a

Roman encampment. He held a portion of the island from 1460 until 1465, but failed to consolidate his position, being opposed by Sir Philip de Carteret, Seigneur of St. Ouen. In 1467, Sir Richard Harliston, Vice Admiral of England, drove out the last of the Norman invaders. The long-suffering islanders thereupon decided to forestall the future use of their homesteads as battleground for any war that might come along. Accordingly, they presented their view of the matter to King Edward IV, who communicated it to Pope Sixtus IV at Rome. Shortly afterwards the Pope issued a Bull of Anathema against all who should thereafter molest the islands. Thus they remained "neutral" until 1689.

Meanwhile the Hardy family had succeeded in establishing its influence in Jersey, taking advantage of all the scuffling, and waxing to a certain mightiness. We hear of another Clement Le Hardy, great-grandson of the first, evidently a resourceful, headstrong and powerful individual. His house, in 1480 or thereabouts, was one of the largest and best on the island. All its windows were secured by iron gratings, in order to frustrate the frequent attacks of unorganized Norman freebooters who in war times delighted to make *razzias* upon the property of the islanders. The outer doors were double, of prodigious thickness, and studded with huge nails. It was situated at St. Martin. Early in the last century it was sold by a Sir Thomas Hardy and was subsequently demolished.

And now the atrocities of Richard III were driving many noble Englishmen across the Channel and into northern France. Great numbers of these fugitive gentlemen passed through Jersey. Clement Le Hardy, associating with them, had formed his own opinions of Richard. Now Henry, Earl of Richmond, of the houses of Gaunt and Lancaster, Pretender to the throne and later Henry VII, had fled from England and was gathering adherents in Brittany.

In 1483 the Duke of Buckingham rose against the King, and Henry decided it was time for him to strike his blow for the crown. He embarked with his retainers. But a storm arose, and his fleet was scattered. The Severn overflowed its banks, to the complete discomfiture of Buckingham. The venture failed completely.

Henry's ship, driven out of its course and separated from the rest of his fleet, sighted the Jersey coast. The Earl landed, alone and unprotected. He found his way to the house at St. Martin, and begged Le Hardy for shelter until he could obtain leave from the French King to re-enter his dominions. Clement offered him all the hospitality at his command, entertained him boldly in spite of Richard's orders for his apprehension, which were published in the island, accompanied by anathemas and threats—not to be too lightly regarded at the time.

Hardy eventually conducted the Earl safely to the Norman shore, at considerable hazard to his own life. As Richmond took his leave of his staunch retainer on the French beach, he gave him his ring as an earnest of future favors, with the words, *"Sic—donec—"* ("Thus —until—"). These words now form one of the mottoes on the Le Hardy arms.

Two years later Henry tried again, this time aided by France. He landed at Milford Haven, defeated Richard

The Life of Thomas Hardy

at Bosworth, and was crowned at Westminster in 1486. Strangely enough for a monarch, he remembered his ring and his promise to his benefactor in Jersey. In 1488 he appointed Clement Le Hardy to be Lieutenant-Governor of the island under Matthew Baker, granted him the Seigneurie de Meleche, and vested him with the office of Chief Magistrate, or Bailiff, for life.

Clement had a son named John. This John was not to be held at home in Jersey, even in the midst of the honors which descended upon the family by reason of his father's bravery and generosity. Like his great-great-grandfather, he was attracted to the north. He may also have felt irked by the physical restrictions of his island home.

And so it happened that John Le Hardy migrated to England, with his wife and children, shortly after his father's elevation. He took up his residence *vers l'ouest*, as the records say, and is reported to have settled somewhere in the valley of the Frome River, perhaps at Toller Wilme. He was the first of the Dorset or "Wessex" Hardys.

Meanwhile the Jersey family carried on the traditions of the great Clement. As adventurous islanders these Le Hardys continued to distinguish themselves, particularly in foreign military service, down to the present day. Their arms were in the last century borne by Lt. Col. Charles Francis Le Hardy of His Majesty's Indian Army. They are

Sable, on a chevron between three escallops, or, as many griffins' heads of the field. Quartering: Azure, a chevron, or, between three cinquefoils, argent, for De Beauvoir: Gules, three

[32]

escallops, or, a crescent for difference, for Dumaresq: and Gules, three escallops, or, a fleur-de-lis, for difference, for Dumaresq. Impaling: Argent, three leaves, vert, for Irving.

Crest: A dexter arm, embowed, in armour, gauntlet, ppr., garnished, or, holding a griffin's head, as in the arms.

Mottoes: Sic Donec. (Above the crest), Le hardy ne querre pas querelle.

John's descendants on the English mainland were many. One line consisted of a long succession of naval heroes. A monument to Sir Thomas Hardy, Kt., Rear-Admiral of the Blue, was erected on the south side of the great entrance in Westminster Abbey by the Rev. Clement Le Hardy, M. A., Rector of St. Peter's. Its inscription reads, in part, as follows:

Near the West door of the Choir, lieth interr'd the body of Sir Thomas Hardy, Kt., who died the 16th of August, 1732, in the 67th year of his age; and, according to the directions of his will, was buried in the same grave with his wife, who died the 28th of April, 1720. . . .

He was bred in the Royal Navy from his youth, and was made a Captain in 1693. In the expedition to Cadiz, under Sir George Rook, he commanded the "Pembrook," and when the Fleet left the Coast of Spain to return to England, he was order'd to Lagos Bay where he got Intelligence of the Spanish Galleons being arrived in the Harbour of Vigo, under convoy of 17 French Men-of-War, commanded by Mons. Chateau Renaud, upon which he sail'd immediately in quest of the English Fleet, and notwithstanding he had been several days separated from it, by his great Diligence and judgment he joyn'd it, and gave the Admiral that intelligence which engag'd him to make the best of his way to Vigo, where all the forementioned Galleons and Men-of-War, were either taken or destroyed. After the success of that Action, the Admiral sent him with an account of it to the

The Life of Thomas Hardy

Queen, who order'd him a considerable Present, and Knighted him; some years afterwards he was made a Rear-Admiral, and receiv'd several other marks of Favour and Esteem from Her Majesty and from her Royal Consort, Prince George of Denmark, Lord High Admiral of England. . . .

Greatest of the whole Hardy naval line, perhaps, was Sir Thomas Masterman Hardy, Bart., of the Portisham branch of the Dorsetshire section of the family. He was Lord Nelson's flag-captain on board the *Victory* at Trafalgar, and was in close personal attendance upon the Admiral on the occasion of his tragic death in the midst of the battle. The scene has received superb poetic treatment in *The Dynasts*. Here is a more matter-of-fact, but touching enough version, taken from the diary of Joseph Farrington:

He said he had conversed with Captn. Hardy of the Victory, who told him that from long habit of walking the deck together, His Steps and those of Lord Nelson were of equal length; that they were walking together (on October 21) & had reached the end of the quarter deck when Lord Nelson stopped & turned suddenly for some purpose; that He proceeded two steps more and turning saw his Lordship fallen on the deck, and two sailors supporting Him; that He went up to his Lordship and expressed his hope that he was not wounded mortally; that Lord Nelson said His back was broke; that then they carried Him down to the cockpit. . . .

Captain Hardy, immortalized by his share in this event, was later made Vice-Admiral, G. C. B., and First Sea Lord of the Admiralty.

The main English branch of the family eventually gravitated towards London. It was lately represented

The Life of Thomas Hardy

through simple illiterate "Hodges." This is untrue. The Hardys have always been, and still are, a class apart from what W. S. Gilbert called "the common country folk" of an "insipid neighborhood." The complete genealogy of the main limbs of the family can be set down only by means of an elaborate and imposing table; only a minute fraction of that great tree has been indicated here. And our Thomas Hardy has always been intensely alive to the quality of the blood of his fathers.

Superficially, this tribal consciousness has cropped out in *The Trumpet-Major* and in *The Dynasts,* in both of which his kinsman (although not his direct ancestor) Sir Thomas Masterman Hardy appears as a *dramatis persona.* Sir Thomas was a Dorset man; he was a Napoleonic hero: these things in themselves would be sufficient to endear him to the Wessex poet. But above all, he was a relative, a Hardy. As such, he was rated glorification, almost deification. The death of Nelson and the attendance of Sir Thomas is in *The Dynasts* portrayed in a series of scenes which stand out as unforgettably thrilling, superlatively pathetic and beautiful even in a framework which is itself full of incomparable thrill, beauty and pathos. They are a *monumentum aere perennius,* a perhaps undeservedly lasting tribute, to the memory of the gallant officer, whose share in the picture was, after all, fundamentally passive. They are the result of a very definite fermentation, for several decades, of varied feelings: love of military pomp and glitter, attachment to the soil over which dead Hardys had pridefully stalked, unavoidable interest in a namesake, deepseated aristocratic arrogance, perhaps only semi-con-

CLEMENT LE HARDY, Jurat, R.C., in 1369 = ... sister of Sire William Lalaque, or Lalazin, who brought him for dower a corn rent of one quarter.

Clement Le Hardy, Jurat, R.C., in 1412 and 1420.

Thomas, Rector of S. Martin in 1432, and Seig. of Melesches in 1446. Living 1463.

Drouet Le Hardy, Jurat, R.C., and Lieut.-Bailly of Jersey in 1444. Living 1463.

Clement Le Hardy, Bailly of Jersey, 1483, Lieut.-Governor, under Matthew Baker, in 1488. Held, in right of his wife, the Fief = Guillemine, d. of John Lempriere, Seig. of Rozel, m. 1456.
Astelle, and Le Fieu de Crap, in S. Clement.

Edward Le Hardy, Jurat, R.C., in 1546, 37 Hen. VIII. = ... d. of . . . . Journeaulx, of La Hougue Boëte.

John, settled in England, as the Pedigrees say, "vers l'Ouest." (At Toller Wilme, co. Dorset? *Vide* Hall. MSS., 427.)

William = Georgette, d. of . . . . Pipon.

Richard, a priest.

Thomas Le Hardy, Constable of S. Martin, 1551 = ... sister of John Hérault, m. before 1556.

James.

Thomas Hardy= . . . . d. of John Perci.

Collette, a ward of John Hérault; of age, June, 1578.

Amice, or Amyas Le Hardy = Mary, d. of Edward Crafford, or Crauford.

Thomas = Catherine, d. of Edmund Perrin, Seig. of Rozel, and Jane Holland, of Dartmouth, his wife.

Mary, m. 23 Jan., 1599 1600. b. 21 Dec , 1621.

Ann, b 17 March, 1593-4.

Jane, or Joan, m = John Le Ré, 18 Dec., 1605, d. or Rey. 5 Oct., 1638.

John Jeunes.

Amice Jeunes, bapt. 27 Jan., 1602-3.

Elizabeth Le Ré, bapt. 6 Feb., 1610-11.

1. Elizabeth, eld d. of John = John Le Hardy, m. 2 May, 1604, = 2. Elizabeth, d. of Philip Dumaresq, Seig. of Vinchelin and Bailly of Jersey, and Collette Dumaresq, his wife. (*Vide* Ped. of Hamptoune.)

Solicitor General, 1613, Jurat, R. C, 1622, Capt. of the Parish of S. Martin. D. there and b. in that parish church, 24 Feb, 1634-5.

De Carteret, widow of Samuel De Beauvoir, b. 1640.

Rachel, only d. and h. of Samuel De Beauvoir, and Elizabeth De Carteret, his wife. Philip Dumaresq, bapt. 5 Feb., 1631-2, Sol.-Gen. of Jersey.

Rachel.

Sarah = Abraham Le Mesire, or Maistre.

Elizabeth, bapt. 6 = Philip Dumaresq, June, 1610. Bur. du Morin. Bur. 30 March, 1651. 20 Mar, 1653-4.

Amice Le Hardy, bapt. 14 Feb., 1604-5, bur. 6 Mar., 1643-5.

John, bapt. 9 Apr., 1606, m. after 20 Feb, 1629-30, and before 14 Dec., 1630, supported = Rachel, only d. and h. of Samuel the Royal Court. His losses were partially recompensed by the Royal Commissioners, 22 June, 1646. He was appointed Sol Gen. of Jersey by Patent, dated 8 Jan., 1633, 10 Charles I., for life, and retained the office during the Commonwealth, having signed the declaration in favour of Charles II. in 1647 as Sol.-Gen. He had a grant of the fief Abbesse de Caen (First Patent dated 29 Nov., 12 William III.) Captain of the parish of S. Martin. Bur. 31 March, 1667.

De Beauvoir, and Elizabeth, De Carteret, his wife. (d. of Ph. De Carteret, Seig. of S. Ouen, and Rachel Poulett). B. before 1616, bur. 16 Aug. 1682.

Samuel, bapt. 18 March, 1637-8, *ob jne.*

Mary, d. of Francis Le Suerr, of S. Helier.

Philip, bapt. 13 Nov., 1639, Bur. 11 Sept., 1640.

Philip, bapt. 22 Oct., 1643, Bur. 5 Oct., 1645.

George, bapt., Sept., 1647, Bur. 3 May, 1661.

Philip, b. 1651, d. 1705, Commissioner of Garrison sons in Guernsey.

Mary, d. of Esaias Filleul, of S. Helier.

Elizabeth, bapt. 10 Oct., 1652.
1. M. D. Olivier.
2. Rev. J. Bonhomme, Rector of S. Peter.

Ann, bapt. 3 March, b. 16 July, 1660.

Jane, bapt. 28 Feb., 1640-1, m. 28 Feb., 1665-6.

Susan, bapt. 22 May, 1642, Bur. 3 Sept., 1642.

Rachel, bapt. 16 Jan., 1644-5, Oct., 1645.

Peter De Beauvoir, Sieur du Bosq, Guernsey.

William De Beauvoir, Sieur du Homet, Guernsey.

Mary.
1. John Suirell.
2. William De Beauvoir, of Guernsey.

Rachel, *ob. insupt.*

Jane.

Francis Amy.

William De Beauvoir, bapt. 12 Oct., 1665, bur. 7 March, 1665-6.

William, living 1698. living 1698.

Jane, living 1698.

Margaret.

John Le Hardy, bapt. 3 March, 1633-4, son and heir, b. 12 Oct., 1655, Jurat, at the Bar, 9 Sept, 1660. Sol.-Gen. of Jersey in 1693. The office had been granted to him by Patent, dated 17 Jan., 12 Charles II., 1661, together with Philip Dumaresq (his first cousin) successively in reversion after the death of his father, John Le Hardy, Captain of the Parish of S. Martin. Bur. 13, Dec., 1692.

Mary, d. of Richard Dumaresq and Jane Hue, his wife. Bur. 4 April, 1694.

Charles, b. 1646 = Mary, d. of Jurat, and Constable of Grouville, d. 1704.

Francis Le Suerr, of S. Helier.

Admiral, the Right = Elizabeth, Hon. Sir Chas. only d. of (Hardy), kt. Josias Pipon, Knight of the Bath, and of the Admiralty, d. 1744.

Elizabeth, only d. of Josias Pipon, chett, Esq., Sec. of the Admiralty.

Esther.

Rev. Charles Dumaresq, Rector of S. John.

1. Mary, d. of B. Tate, Esq.

Sir Charles, Kt. Admiral = 2. Catherine, only of the White, Com.-in-Chief d. of Temple of the Channel Fleet in 1779. Stanyan, Esq.

William, living 1698. living 1698.

Charlotte.

Elizabeth.

Christopher Hake, Esq.

Catherine.

Arthur Anneley, Esq., of Bletchingdon, Oxon.

John, Rear-Admiral, d 1796.

Edward Le Hardy, Commander in the African Company, d. 1723.

Josiah Hardy, Consul at Cadiz, d. 1790.

George Hardy.

Charles.

Temple, Lieut., R.N.

Susan.

Harriet, 6th d. of Sir Thos. D'Arth, Bart.

The roots of Hardy's family tree. From Payen-Payne's *Armorial of Jersey*, 1862.

scious, but doubtless intensified by enforced comparative lowliness.

Still more superficial indications of this can easily be found in Hardy's directly expressed opinions of the Wessex underlings. Certainly he never writes of them as one of them, particularly in his frankly detached, if sympathetic, article, *The Dorsetshire Labourer.* He examines their reactions with the disinterested feelings of a chemist making a quantitative analysis.

Nor did he ever see anything in his parents to permit him to identify himself with the tillers and villagers. The "Wessex dialect," although recognized as a language with claims to legitimacy perhaps superior to those of London English, was nevertheless strictly *verboten* within the walls of his birthplace.

It is of course true, and Hardy has himself frankly admitted, that his own immediate forbears were no longer personages of great importance, even locally. His father's own particular line had suffered something of a tragic fall from high estate perhaps analogous to the deterioration of the D'Urbervilles in the novel. This point, however, must not be pressed too weightily. Hardy has repeatedly warned biographers against the dangerous and "impertinent" procedure of identifying him or his associates too closely with the figures of his imagination, tempting and half-truthful as this may often be. It must be done very gingerly, if at all. One must remember the posthumous evil it has wrought in the past upon the fame of Sappho of Lesbos and Will Langland of Shropshire.

Hardy's father, for instance, had decidedly not fallen

as low as old Durbeyfield, the town drunkard. Nor can he in any way be related to the plebeian father of Stephen Smith of *A Pair of Blue Eyes,* a character actually suggested to Hardy by a workman in his father's employ. Tragic feeling may run through the family, but it cannot be the instinctive fatalism of the peasant. Hardy's so-called "pessimism" is emphatically of the intellectual and heroic type, born of physical comfort and reflective thought. His immediate relatives, it is true, had to work in order to exist; sometimes even the women. His sister at one time taught school in Dorchester. Yet there is no reason to suppose that, as a group, these Hardys longed for past ease and a vast share of fleshpots and affluence, consoling themselves finally with an acquiescent and renunciative determinism.

The poet's father was a master-builder by trade, employing about ten men on an average, and lived in circumstances that may fairly be called prosperous. He was able, at any rate, to afford special efforts for the early education of his son. A Joseph Poorgrass knows nothing of French governesses. That, in point of culture, the builder belonged to the extremely modest class of which the band of church-musicians in *Under the Greenwood Tree* is representative, is an indefensible thesis. Hardy has found occasion to resent with some bitterness this erroneous assumption, prevalent sometimes even among his intimates. The Norman blood of Clement the elder has been stirred to a cruel ebullience under certain circumstances.

* *

*

Origins (1360-1772)

The derivation of Hardy's mother presents a picture of different composition. If his father's line demonstrates a natural descent from Norman nobility to west-country bourgeoisie, his mother's indicates a steady, unvarying adherence to the class and attainments of the solid, intelligent, independent English yeomanry.

Her people were the Swetmans and the Childses, two groups which have often intermarried, and have for centuries lived only in the neighborhood of Melbury Osmond, the "King's Hintock" of Hardy's "Wessex," a picturesque old village on the plateau which spans the Frome Valley and the Vale of Blackmoor. Here the proliferation of life streams upwards from the rich soil with unquenchable vigor.

While the Hardys adhered to their ruffle-sleeved King during the Civil Wars, the Swetman and Childs families were stanch Parliamentarians and Roundheads. They were energetic small landholders, self-sufficient, independent, occasionally even defiant, of the surrounding Lords of the Manors. They may be traced with certainty as far back as 1635; beyond that the ancestral lines are somewhat blurred.

The old Swetman house in Melbury Osmond was in later times the only pre-Elizabethan structure in the neighborhood; its windows were mullioned in the Sixteenth Century manner. It was later sold. Hardy himself, in *The Duke's Reappearance,* has related a characteristic family tradition connected with this dwelling. At the time of Monmouth's Rebellion, one Christopher Swetman lived there, as head of the family. A man of some spirit, he was secretly in sympathy with the cause of the Duke. The night following Monmouth's defeat, a cloaked and spurred gentleman, a mud-spattered cavalier, knocked at Christopher's door. He declined to disclose his identity, but Christopher respected his incognito and gave him shelter, even as the fleeing Henry of Richmond had been sheltered by Clement Le Hardy. But the unfortunate Duke found it impossible to resist the charms of the pretty Swetman daughters. Honest Christopher discovered him making love to one of them in the garden and ordered him to be on his way. A few days later news came that Monmouth was apprehended and beheaded in the Tower, but not before Swetman had observed a mysterious figure removing the hidden Ducal trappings from his cupboard. It was thus that the Swetmans, because of their bourgeois horror for courtly customs, missed what was perhaps an opportunity to rise in the world similar to the one which came to the Jersey Hardys in the Fifteenth Century. That tradition, according to Hardy, has been handed down from Swetman to Swetman for more than two hundred years, although the Childs family also lays claim to it.

Hardy's grandmother was born in 1772 and lived until 1857. Thus, until he was seventeen years old, the poet had the advantage of sitting at this ancient's lady's feet and listening to many an obscure legend, humorous or pathetic, from her lips. For she was, by all accounts, a storehouse of local stories and pictures, and not at all averse to retailing them. Her garrulity, if such it was, served Hardy well in his later efforts to create living images in prose and verse of the swiftly vanishing color of his Dorset environment. For he retained in his exder age. And yet—one must remember what curious pranks, to our thinking, our ancients in their eighties can sometimes play. They live in a world apart; their standards are often more flexible, more ethically "enlightened" and "progressive" than those of the most ardent youthful anarchs and iconoclasts.

If his grandmother thus provided the raw materials for his cold X-ray studies of character under the bombardment of environment and circumstance, it was Hardy's mother who stimulated his earliest impulses to translate them into artistic entities. This mother was a woman who had found it possible to add immeasurably to her perhaps meagre experience of life by losing herself in the perusal of what was best in the literature of the past. She indulged a taste for the classical Latin poets, notably Virgil, and for French romances and tragedies. She was ambitious in a literary way.

There can be little doubt that that ambition, in a lady of her circumstances and position, was not untouched by a bit of literary snobbishness. Her artistic polish could be little more than a *patina* on the surface of her personality, and her enthusiasm for Horace, Catullus and the English Cavalier poets could scarcely reach down deeply enough to disturb her subsoil of simple yeoman sentiment and idealism.

The sharp hatred of class prejudice, also, that acrid distaste for polite society which permeates *The Hand of Ethelberta,* is just the type of social liberalism that almost invariably accompanies the "literary" flair of the ardent amateur—and this trait in the novelist is distinctly traceable to the elder Mrs. Hardy. It is, in these

days, a reliable indication of the worshipper-from-afar
of the *belles-lettrist*. In this case it was founded on the
deepest basic sympathy with the sturdy franklin-class,
on an understanding of Hodge and his country that had
its roots in inherited feelings rather than in acquired
syllogisms. The country yeomanry has been called the
backbone of the English nation's character. Although
this observation has been repeated so often as to become
an article of the British Credo, there is nevertheless
some truth in it.

Late in his life the poet enshrined the more tender aspects of his spiritual debt to his mother in the poem
called *The Roman Road* (included in his *Time's Laughingstocks*) :

> The Roman Road runs straight and bare
> As the pale parting-line in hair
> Across the heath. And thoughtful men
> Contrast its days of Now and Then,
> And delve, and measure, and compare;
>
> Visioning on the vacant air
> Helmed legionaries, who proudly rear
> The Eagle, as they pace again
>> The Roman Road.
>
> But no tall brass-helmed légionnaire
> Haunts it for me. Uprises there
> A mother's form upon my ken,
> Guiding my infant steps, as when
> We walked that ancient thoroughfare,
>> The Roman Road.

*   *

*

LIEUT COLONEL CHARLES FRANCIS LE HARDY.

H. M. INDIAN ARMY.

Coat-of-arms of the Hardy family. From Payen-Payne's *Armorial of Jersey*, 1862. Sable on a chevron between three escallops, or as many griffins' heads of the field. Quartering: Azure, a chevron, or, between three cinquefoils, argent, for De Beauvoir: Gules, three escallops, or a crescent for difference, for Dumaresq: and Gules, three escallops, or a fleur-de-lis, for difference, for Dumaresq. Impaling: Argent, three leaves, vert, for Irving. Crest: A dexter arm, embowed, in armour, gauntlet, ppr., garnished, or holding a griffin's head, as in the arms.

Origins (1360-1772)

Through his mother, then, Hardy gained his affection for the soil and its creatures, his subjective appreciation for their emotions and reactions, his fiery strain of humanitarianism, his artistic taste, in the superficial sense of the expression. This emancipated countryman-spirit of his can account for the craftsman in him, but never for the imaginative psychologist. It can account for the ambitious writer, determined to make his mark in the London reviews, but never for the cosmic poet. It can account for many of his affections, perhaps, but not for his detached realization of all-too-human motives. The responsibility for these latter endowments rests largely with the French nobility transmitted through Hardy the master-builder. Partially overshadowing the yeoman's spiritual harmony with the commoner and the peasant is the overlord-adventurer's intolerance of the villein's naïveté, the occasional cruel sneer in his attitude towards the serf.

The combination of these two inherited planes, each with its own particular breadth as well as restriction, enabling the poet to view and to criticise his world objectively while experiencing it to the full subjectively, has had a mighty share in making Hardy the full-dimensioned genius he is.

*　　*

*

But the necessary third dimension, to provide body, solidity, and the feel and flavor of genuine reality to the quality of Hardy's poetic, is perforce discoverable only in his environment. That "Wessex" which first determined him, only to be itself determined later on by the child of its moods, demands a very particular consideration on the part of the biographer. The fourth dimension, finally (Time, or Chance, or "Crass Casualty") naturally follows in the sequel of events.

CHAPTER III

The Soil (. . . 1850)

From this self-contained place rose in stealthy silence tall stems of smoke, which the eye of imagination could trace downward to their root on quiet hearth-stones festooned overhead with hams and flitches. It was one of those sequestered spots outside the gates of the world where may usually be found more meditation than action, and more passivity than meditation; where reasoning proceeds on narrow premises, and results in inferences wildly imaginative; yet where, from time to time, dramas of a grandeur and unity truly Sophoclean are enacted in the real, by virtue of the concentrated passions and closely knit interdependence of the lives therein.

BY many a literary incantation such as this has Thomas Hardy called into being and summoned up before his readers the Genii of his native country. Or, viewed from a slightly different angle, "Wessex" has been to him a vast stage upon which things both animate and inanimate have been woven together in comic and tragic patterns, as the winds of chance blew upon them, or as causal chains, stretching infinitely into the past, have determined them.

"Wessex" has been to Hardy primarily a land of associations. He never walked through it saying, "So, and so, and so, might events have complicated themselves—thus, and thus, in such a place." He rather imagined, "Here tragedies did actually play themselves out, and did actually lead on, and will always lead on, to further

tragedies, in the manner foreordained by the Will."
Under such a mental attitude the terrain came to life.
Spirits dead, living, unborn, invested every stone, every
tree, everything raised by the hand of man. The real in-
volved itself inextricably with the spectre of the real.

Under such an emotional radiation, also, the past and
the present must of necessity have become deeply in-
volved with each other and interblended. The soil and
its fruit: the ground itself, its vegetation, its animal life,
its human product or parasite whose activities here and
there resulted in physical denudations and excrescences:
roads and ditches, churches and dwellings—all these have
played both a real and a transcendental rôle in Hardy's
cosmos. Hardy himself must be taken as a part of it, too.

"Wessex" can not be considered, then, merely as it re-
produces itself photographically through human sensory
reactions today. Its history must be invoked to cast over
it something of the romantic glow in which Hardy's
imagination has thrived. And not merely its conventional modern history alone, important as this may be,
but even its geology and its prehistory.

*   *

*

Fishy beings of low development, then dragon forms
and clouds of flying reptiles, then shadowy, sinister
crocodilian outlines: alligators and other uncouth shapes,
culminating in the colossal lizard, iguanodon—these
beasties we must first imagine as peopling the more ancient geological deposits of southwestern England.
Hardy's Henry Knight, hanging against the Cliff With-

The Soil (. . . 1850)

out A Name, sees them all. Then huge elephantine forms, the mastodon, the hippopotamus, the tapir, antelopes of monstrous size, the megatherium and the mylodon, also huge-billed birds and swinish creatures as large as horses. Such an uncouth rout of inhabitants constitutes the fantastically romantic animate prologue for the appearance of the first Wessex men: fierce creatures, living in mean times, although perhaps no meaner than the present. Clothed in hides of beasts and carrying, for defence and attack, huge clubs and pointed spears, they "rose from the rock like the phantoms before the doomed Macbeth. They lived in hollows, woods and mud huts— perhaps in caves of the neighboring rocks." Dig down a few feet anywhere in Dorsetshire, and you will find the mute evidences of these bizarre races. Nineteenth Century science has bared them all to the vision of the romancer.

There followed wars and tumults. Tribes grew into nations. Life, then as now, tasted bitter; still men drank deeply of it, prolonged its deceptive hopes as effectively as they could. They attacked their neighbors, and erected elaborate defenses against them. Mai Dun, the result of years of toil, lakes of sweat and blood, reared up its grim ponderosity over the teeming green wilderness of the Frome Valley. Hundreds of tiny beings, Lilliputians in comparison with the colossal magnitude of their materialized ambitions, swarmed over the country in little bands and flocks, driven on by forces they could never understand.

Inspired by their awesome apprehension of a malignant, though perhaps only indifferent, spirit, brooding over their destiny, they carved huge boulders into symmetrical forms and erected monoliths and triliths. Some they dragged over to Salisbury Plain and there established their Temple to the Sun: vast concentric circles of stone, burning in the fierce heat of noonday, chill as death at midnight. Here at Stonehenge their vague terrors prompted them to offer the blood of their own sons and daughters to appease their instinctive and traditional concepts of a stern and outraged "justice." ("I think you are lying," says Angel to Tess, "on the very altar on which they offered their sacrifices." . . .)

The Wessex realm became a vaguely circumscribed district, bounded on the east and north by a line running from where Portsmouth now stands, over towards the sources of the Thames, and to the west, clear to Land's End. Here hoary legendary British kings ruled their rude people with passion and caprice, here bards chanted of blood and demons—while far to the southeast, along the shores of the Mediterranean, people were developing law, art, literature and philosophy. It is pleasant to dream, once remarked Hardy, that in some spot in the extensive tract named "Egdon" may be the hearth of that traditionary King of Wessex, Ina, afterwards named Lear. The storms that now howl about the ears of the belated nightly wayfarer on these barren moors, at any rate, are the identical tempests that puffed their cheeks and mercilessly goaded on the white-haired old monarch, a pathetic figure, mad, quite mad, a victim of man's eternal inhumanity to man.

Relentless legions of the Roman Cæsars next left the imprint of their steel-shod heels over the country.

The Soil (. . . 1850)

Polished, gleaming metal, straight ranks and files of soldiery, shouting centurions, aristocratic Imperial officers —the harsh, precise machine mowed down all that stood in its path. Efficiency invaded the wilderness, for the first time—but not the last. The Britons were driven back, or enslaved, or carried off to Italy. Camps were laid out, their sites chosen scientifically. Bridges spanned the streams. Roads, hard as metal, white as marble, straight as spear-shafts, pierced through virgin woodlands.

The camps grew into towns, where people lived the orderly, virtuous lives of pioneers extending the frontiers of their nation. A precise language, with neatly interlocking combinations of long and short vowels and consonants, beautifully inflected, prevailed—a language which contained miraculous words that represented not only things and actions but generalized concepts. Self-consciousness and rigid logical thinking sought, with temporary success, to impress the face of the island, upon which time had thus far written but a shallow story, when all was told.

Justice was administered, business methods were applied to human intercourse. Regulated amusements provided controllable outlets for spirits that naturally and periodically craved excitement and stimulation. Amphitheatres were dug out of the verdant hillsides. Here were staged races, combats, pompous solemn processionals, perhaps even the comedies of Plautus and the tragedies of Seneca. Two miles—two thousand Roman paces —north of Mai Dun, sprang up the capital city of the Imperial province.

The Life of Thomas Hardy

A few hundred years passed—and then there remained but little more indication of this brazen impact than one can discover there today. Durnovaria became Durnover Field. The dry bones of the conquerors and masters were enclosed in the warm but indifferent embraces of the untamable soil. Pavements of tiles were overgrown with sod. Sheep grazed within Maumbry Rings; the slopes that had rung with triumphal shouts now protected fleecy backs from the gelid November winds. Hadrian's soldiery lay buried in shallow graves, their knees drawn up to their chins; herdsmen gaped dumbly at the curious upturned "skellintons."

From the east came Germanic marauders. The autochthonous Keltic warriors were driven further and further back—over into Wales, up into the hills of Scotland. Some of the chieftains held out in their stony strongholds, miraculously parrying all onslaughts until they were exterminated, and thus the Arthurian legends were born. Blond Saxons, prevailing by numbers and savagery, built their settlements. The Cyning, with his grave Witenagemot and his shouting thegnas, at last succeeded in impressing the enduring countenance of Wessex, the land of the West-Saxons, with the spiritual aspect it bears today. Their Teutonic language, called the "Englisce spræce," unlocking its word-hoards, resounded through the raftered halls and the cultivated fields, to remain there practically unchanged by the vicissitudes of many centuries. Also their pagan Nordic superstitions, but thinly overlaid, eventually, with Christian celestial machinery. Wyrd, the inscrutable personification of Destiny, transplanted from Scandinavia, found

The Soil (. . . 1850)

Its new habitation much to Its liking. It awakened the fossilized monsters and dragons into a second existence; they lived again, as brooding shadows, magical, mysterious, terrible.

Hardy Danes, fiery and volatile people, charged over from the southeast coast; their raids harried the land. Æthelstan, Ælfred, Æthelred, sober kings and true, spent their lives pruning their spear-hedges in continuous campaigns of defence. Mounds that had served the Stone-Age men, the Britons and the Romans in turn, were again used as barriers against the invading marauders. Peace approached on belated pinions.

Missionaries had arrived from Rome; the barbarians were gradually won over to baptism and to lip-service of the Lord, His Risen Son, the Virgin Mother and the Holy Saints. Church towers bore aloft the Sign of the Cross. But Wyrd, unconquered, brooding, nursing its monsters in the hearts of the land-folk, smiled grimly through it all.

Henceforward the history of Wessex becomes the history of the English nation. The Dukes of Normandy, having vanquished the last of the Saxon monarchs, imposed their feudal lordship over the country. Ecclesiastical architecture of the Perpendicular type dominated the towns.

For more than seven centuries, this Anglo-Norman civilization held sway. The Hardys had arrived and were proliferating. The Swetmans and the Childses, by dint of Habsburgian intermarrying, had populated the heart of Wessex, covered it with substantial barns and houses of stone, built to endure for many generations.

The Life of Thomas Hardy

The Nineteenth Century crept nearer. Across the Channel, off the southwest coast, a great Gallic nation was in the throes of popular turmoil, social upheaval and political rebirth. England throbbed sympathetically: everywhere, throughout the land, patrols of scarlet-coated military were on view, passing to and fro, in and out of billets and barracks, as foreign campaigns swiftly followed one another. Hanoverian gaiety, in the person and the court of the Third George, invaded the seaside towns. Weymouth resounded with martial music and with sprightly, rippling dances whose echoes were sensed even in the quiet villages of the interior. But it was a liveliness impregnated with anxiety. The Ogre of Corsica, savage "Boney," threatened to land his thousands of devils from his fleet of flat-bottomed rafts; his name was coupled with the Evil One's; his image terrorized children into obedience. Beacons were prepared as signals of the dreaded landing, on the summits of the ancient Dorset barrows. Recruiting and impressing for Lord Nelson's navy affrighted the mothers and lovers of lusty youngsters.

The even flow of rural life was scarcely disturbed by the tumult, however. Foreign affairs, being invisible, even if real, were lumped together with all the other real but invisible things: with ogres and witches, with dragons and magic potions. The shepherds, pine-planters, ploughmen, furze-cutters, dairymen, went about their daily tasks just as they had for centuries. Ballads and folk-tales were still transmitted orally, substantially the same, in content and handling, as they had been in pre-Elizabethan days.

The Soil (. . . 1850)

The country girls and swains danced around the pole on May Day; on Christmas Eve, when the oxen were supposed to be on their knees in the stables, the waits went about chanting old noels; conjurors were consulted at dead of night; the old play of St. George, beginning with the lines,

> Here come I, a Turkish knight,
> Who learnt in Turkish land to fight . . .

periodically slaked the popular thirst for the drama; people who were intensely disliked, or whose manner of living provoked criticism, were subjected to "skimmity-riding"; to pierce a waxen image of one's enemy with needles and to melt it over a fire while reciting the Lord's Prayer backwards three times was considered equivalent to murder and damnation.

"Superstitions linger longest on these heavy soils," Hardy has remarked of the central Vale of Blackmore. "Having once been forest, at this shadowy time it seemed to assert something of its old character, the far and the near being blended, and every tree and tall hedge making the most of its presence. The harts that had been hunted here; the witches that had been pricked and ducked; the green-spangled fairies;—the place teemed with beliefs in them still, and they formed an impish multitude now."

Thus paganism lingered on through the early part of the last century. The folk were church-goers, of course, and their speech was punctuated by frequent turns of phrase out of the Bible and Prayer Book. Their clergy forced them to maintain the proper respect for the cere-

[55]

monies that had been imported, established and adhered to by their fathers for hundreds of years. In church they professed much, but believed very little; in the dim chambers of conjurors they professed little, but believed much —and that with shaking and dread. Fetichism ran far ahead of traditional ritual and dogmatism.

* *

*

Such was the Wessex that Hardy loved from the earliest to the latest days of his life. He loved the country both for itself and for its associations, but he loved the countryman for himself alone. Hardy's peasant was, as Lionel Johnson justly remarked, neither a Strephon nor a Hodge, neither Arcadian nor clown; he was just as he was. Yet his possibilities were unlimited. Twice, at least, did Hardy give recognition to his recognition of these potentialities: in one of his rare interviews, signed by a "quondam country parson" in 1892, and in *Tess*. Here is a composite rendition of both:

"As to 'Hodge,' I have never met him. The conventional farm-folk of the imagination—personified by the pitiable figure known as Hodge—are soon obliterated from the consciousness of the just observer. At close quarters no Hodge is to be seen. At first, it is true, rustic ideas, modes and surroundings may appear retrogressive and unmeaning. But living on there, day after day, the acute sojourner becomes conscious of a new aspect in the spectacle. Without any objective change whatever, variety takes the place of monotonousness. As the folk become intimately known, they begin to differentiate

"Egdon Heath"—Puddletown Heath, near
Bockhampton, Dorsetshire. From an
aquatint by John Everett.

The Soil (. . . 1850)

themselves as in a chemical process. The typical and unvarying Hodge ceases to exist. He has been disintegrated into a number of varied fellow-creatures—beings of many minds, beings infinite in difference; some happy, many serene, a few depressed, one here and there bright even to genius, some stupid, others wanton, others austere; some mutely Miltonic, some potentially Cromwellian; into men who have private views of each other, as the observer has of his friends; who can applaud or condemn each other, amuse or sadden themselves by the contemplation of each other's foibles or vices; men everyone of whom walks in his own individual way the road to dusty death.''

These people of Hardy's, one may be reasonably sure, composed the actual Wessex "backbone," at least until about 1860. Additional illumination of a brilliant quality is thrown over this picture by Hardy's remarks on the country clergy. The fact that he delivered them to a "quondam parson" may have colored them somewhat charitably, but still he sounded the note of sincerity when he said:

"Great credit is due to the parson, who, in my opinion, does much to keep up the interest in these quiet villages. It would be a thousand pities that such men, educated, sympathetic, original-minded as many of them are, should be banished by looming difficulties of dogma, and the villages given over to the narrow-mindedness and the lack of charity of some lower class of teacher."

"How, then," asked his interlocutor, "do you explain the great dislike that exists in the rural breast for the parson?" To which Hardy replied:

The Life of Thomas Hardy

"I think he is so disliked, where he is disliked, more on account of his friendship with the squire and the powers that be; because he teaches a theology which they cannot square with the facts of life. The Liberationist Society are on the wrong tack; let them liberate the parson from his theology, not the parish from the parson."

Throughout his literary career, indeed, Hardy continually recognized the great power of the parson for both good and evil in the community. His first picture of the pastor, in *Desperate Remedies,* is a consistently sympathetic one. Contrasted with this presentation of the clergyman as a force which worked for good in the physical and spiritual life of the district is the portrait of Mr. Swancourt in *A Pair of Blue Eyes,* a petty dignitary whose social prejudices and altogether selfish propensities have much to do with the hastening on of the catastrophe of the story, and constitute proper vehicles for a cynical presentation of the futility and occasional malignity of the representatives of the Church. The more neutral characterizations of Angel Clare's father in *Tess* and of Parson Maybold in *Under the Greenwood Tree* are indicative of Hardy's more tolerant moods when reacting to the country clergy—although the picture is scarcely complete without the addition of that biting "satire of circumstance," *In Church,* a truly diabolical, sardonic glimpse:

> "And now to God the Father," he ends,
> And his voice thrills up to the topmost tiles:
> Each listener chokes as he bows and bends,
> And emotion pervades the crowded aisles.

The Soil (. . . 1850)

Then the preacher glides to the vestry door,
And shuts it, and thinks he is seen no more.

The door swings softly ajar meanwhile,
And a pupil of his in the Bible class
Who adores him as one without gloss or guile,
Sees her idol stand with a satisfied smile
And re-enact at the vestry glass
Each pulpit gesture in deft dumb-show
That had moved the congregation so.

And from first to last the poet exercised no patience
with the theology taught by the wearers of holy orders.

In his enthusiasm for the countryman Hardy has often
been compared with Wordsworth, but that his understanding of the native heart and mind was infinitely superior to that of the great optimistic nature-poet has
been shown rather conclusively by the great esteem and
friendliness that the farm and working people of his own
district have always felt for him. According to "John
O'London," he "sees a peasant culture from his own
art, and the Wessex villagers greet him as their Pros-
pero, whose staff must one day be broken and buried,
but whose book will never be drowned." It will be remembered that the country folk of the Lake district liter-
ally ran before the approach of Wordsworth (meditative,
benevolent, wordy and moral sage that he was), who, for
all his sympathy, seems to have lacked a real understanding of the man of the soil. His philosophy of the rustic
heart was one drawn largely out of books and easy-chair
meditation rather than from the actual experience with
material contact with his clouted subjects. Hardy's sym-

pathy, on the other hand, was always that of the fellow-worker and fellow-sufferer, no matter how clear-sighted and aristocratic he remained within himself.

*　　*

*

The Dorset language itself has been enshrined with both exactness and artistic feeling in the "dialect" verse written by the Rev. William Barnes of Winterbourne. Hardy's interests in the past and present of the country, of the people and of the speech of Wessex, as well as in the art of poetry in and for itself, were united in his enthusiasm for the figure and work of this remarkable poet.

Born in 1800, Barnes had lived his whole life among the Wessex folk; like Hardy he had become enamored of the ancient dialect, had learnt to penetrate into the highways and byways of the rural heart, and, like Hardy again, had easily won the admiration of his country parishioners through his deep sympathy and keen insight into their ways, which he could at will adopt as his own, and make the feelings and expressions of the peasant a part of himself. It is said that his most appreciative audiences did not consist of cultivated readers, charmed with the "quaintness" and "naïveté" of his dialect lyrics, but of the users of the dialect themselves, delighted with the truthfulness and naturalness of his poetry and of his manner of reading it.

Although well equipped to apply himself to the evolution, grammar and etymology of the Dorset language with all the scientific intensity of the professional philologer, he seems to have been able to retain the simple

The Soil (. . . 1850)

point of view of the uncultured Dorset rustic and to associate with him on terms of the greatest familiarity. In this respect he and Hardy were kindred spirits. His best creative work, the *Poems of Rural Life,* appeared in 1879, and drew forth an enthusiastic review from Hardy in the *New Quarterly Magazine* for October of that year—it was the only review that Hardy ever wrote. When Barnes died in 1886, Hardy wrote the eloquent obituary article in the *Athenæum.* The following poetic tribute can also be discovered in Hardy's *Moments of Vision.* It is called *The Last Signal* (Oct. 11, 1886)—*A Memory of William Barnes:*

Silently I footed by an uphill road
That led from my abode to a spot yew-boughed;
Yellowly the sun sloped down to westward,
And dark was the east with cloud.

Then, below the shadow of that livid sad east,
Where the light was least, and a gate stood wide,
Flashed back the fire of the sun that was facing it,
Like a brief blaze on that side.

Looking hard and harder I knew what it meant—
The sudden shine sent from the livid east scene;
It meant the west mirrored by the coffin of my friend there,
Turning to the road from his green,

To take his last journey forth—he who in his prime
Trudged so many a time from that gate athwart the land!
Thus a farewell to me he signalled on his grave-way,
As with a wave of his hand.

(Winterborne-Came Path)

The Life of Thomas Hardy

While it would be very difficult indeed to exaggerate the purely literary influence of Barnes, especially over Hardy's early activity as a lyric poet, it must be clearly understood at the outset that of intellectual influence there was practically none. Hardy's consistently revolutionary and irreconcilable attitude both towards the organized social world and towards the first principles manifesting themselves in the tragic features of life found no inspiration or nourishment in the devout and mellow mood of reverent acceptance running through all of the clergyman's work. He himself hinted at this fundamental distinction between the two general viewpoints in the obituary article:

Unlike Burns, Béranger, and other poets of the people, Mr. Barnes never assumed the high conventional style; and he entirely leaves alone ambition, pride, despair, defiance and others of the grander passions which move mankind great and small. His rustics are, as a people, happy people, and very seldom feel the sting of the rest of modern mankind—the disproportion between the desire for serenity and the power of obtaining it. One naturally thinks of Crabbe in this connexion; but though they touch at points, Crabbe goes much further than Barnes in questioning the justice of circumstance.

Great as is the gulf between Barnes and Crabbe, it is far exceeded by that between Crabbe and Hardy. Even the country-folk among Hardy's characters often give expression to opinions which smack of the Satanic rather than the traditional view of the world and its Creator. Hardy gave generous praise to Barnes, however, for having contented himself with the presentation of the simple attitudes of the wielders of the hoe. A significant para-

The Soil (. . . 1850)

graph in the preface which he wrote in 1908 for the *Select
Poems* of Barnes reads:

> Dialect, it may be added, offered another advantage to him as
> a writer, whatever difficulties it may have for strangers who try
> to follow it. Even if he often used the dramatic form of peasant
> speakers as a pretext for the expression of his own mind and
> experiences—which cannot be doubted—yet he did not always
> do this, and the assumed characters of husbandman and ham-
> leteer enabled him to elude in his verse those dreams and specu-
> lations that cannot leave alone the mystery of things—possibly
> an unworthy mystery and disappointing if solved, though one
> that has a harrowing fascination for many poets,—and helped
> him to fall back on dramatic truth, by making his personages ex-
> press the notions of life prevalent in their sphere.

There can certainly be no doubt about the harrowing
fascination that the mystery of things has always possessed for Hardy, and none about the vigorous and outspoken way he sometimes chose to express his personal
reaction to it.

Widely separated as the two poets were in the matter
of faith and its expression in their literary works, they
approached each other very closely when they turned the
eye of sympathetic observation upon the simple people
and the simple details of country life. Here we find the
effect of the older man's kindly attitude to have been a
mighty influence over the young iconoclast. Outside of
his admiration for recognized masters, such as the Greek
tragic dramatists, the Old Testament poets, Shakespeare,
Shelley, Goethe and Schopenhauer, the only great literary enthusiasm displayed by Hardy was for the unas-
suming work of Barnes—and this despite the self-evident

differences between their fundamental ideas. The sympathy between the two, therefore, in those matters where sympathy really existed, must have been very strong indeed.

With regard to the most obvious bond that connected the two, namely, their attachment to and employment of the dialect, a cursory investigation reveals the fact that, superficially at least, their use of the native tongue differed. The Barnes poems require a glossary, such as that supplied by Hardy, for the reader unacquainted with the dialect, while the dialogue of Hardy's rustics can be readily followed by anyone who can read standard English. Barnes aimed at much closer and more exact reproduction, orthographically, of the pure dialect: he consistently printed "z" for the voiced "s"-sound (the effect of which was not intended to be humorous), and "v" for the voiced "f"; and he used many more words found only in Dorset and not in London English.

Except for the early Wessex ballad, *The Bride-Night Fire*, or, as it was first called, *The Fire at Tranter Sweatley's*, in which he came closest to a real reproduction of the Barnes matter and expression, Hardy used the dialect in far freer fashion. For this further corruption of what was considered by many only a corruption of the accepted language, he was severely criticised. He answered his critics in his letter to the *Athenæum* of November 30, 1878, in which he protested that his aim was primarily to depict men and women and their natures rather than their dialect forms, and that an accurate phonetic transcription of their actual speech would only emphasize a grotesqueness really nonexistent. Thus he

The Soil (. . . 1850)

justified what may still seem a curious compromise between scientifically naturalistic speech-reproduction and unscientific cross-fertilization of two distinct languages.

This inexactness and license in the employment of what was so carefully, accurately and jealously recorded in the work of Barnes was amply atoned for by Hardy's greater richness in the use of rural idioms and by his very generous paraphrases of characteristic, revealing turns of speech. Barnes, on the other hand, frequently forsook the simplicity and the naïve rustic euphuism so delightfully indulged in by Hardy's countrymen, and decked out their language with the cut and dried flowers of traditional book-rhetoric. The flowers in the speech of William Worm, Joseph Poorgrass, Grandfer Cantle and their associates are always fresh, spontaneous, and of the wild and uncultivated variety. But although Hardy never violated the peasant character himself, he thus defended Barnes's practice:

What is the use of saying, as has been said of Barnes, that compound epithets like "the blue-hill'd worold," "the white horn'd cow," "the grey-topp'd heights of Paladore," are a high-handed enlargement of the ordinary ideas of the fieldfolk into whose mouths they are put? These things are justified by the art of every age when they can claim to be, as here, singularly precise and beautiful definitions of what is signified; which in these instances, too, apply with double force to the deeply tinged horizon, to the breed of kine, to the aspect of Shaftesbury Hill, characteristic of the Vale within which most of his revelations are enshrined.

Both authors were united on insisting upon the view that the Dorset dialect was, and always had been, a real language and not a corruption; but it should be noted that, as Hardy pointed out in his preface, Barnes strained at times the capacity of dialect in his "aim at closeness of phrase to his vision, and went wilfully outside the dramatization of peasant talk." He went on to observe, "Whether or no, by a felicitous instinct, he does at times break into sudden irregularities in the midst of his subtle rhythms and measures, as if feeling rebelled against further drill. Then his self-consciousness ends, and his naturalness is saved."

The two principles of poetic diction mentioned above and admired by Hardy in Barnes were never forsaken by the younger poet. The aim at "closeness of phrase to vision" is a characteristic of Hardy's verse from the earliest of his *Wessex Poems* to the latest of his *Late Lyrics*. Likewise the poet's liberty to break into sudden irregularities of metre when feeling rebels against drill, although not frequently indulged in by Barnes, is a significant quality to find winning the admiration of Hardy. It seems to indicate a certain duality of personality in him as a writer: on the one hand, the tinge of austere reaction which made him an admirer of the smooth flow, the liquid verse and the common ideas of the Cavalier lyrists; on the other hand, the frequent contrasting display of metric irregularity and a deliberate sacrifice of melody to the pungency of the thought to be expressed.

The poems of Barnes are chiefly distinguished by their extreme regularity of metre, their great beauty of language, their smooth and skilful handling of words and by their fine idyllic quality, sometimes mingled with pathos, but hardly ever with the sting of real tragedy.

The Soil (. . . 1850)

The events portrayed are those most common in rural life: courtings, weddings and deaths; and in their portrayal dramatic fire and tension are nearly always absent. For their quaint and felicitous expression of a poet's real joy in the countryside, in the approach of spring, in familiar scenes and faces and in the cheerful winter's fireside, these poems really deserve to be widely known.

The broad dialect can be observed at its best in *The Gre't Woak Tree That's in the Dell.* Here the effect of beauty and pathos is admirably rendered by images at once simple and meaningful. A typical Hardy-motif is sounded in *Minden House,* which tells of a youth's falling in love with a farmer's daughter, and closes as follows:

> Vor Time had now a-showed en dim
> The jay it had in store vor him. . . .
> An' when he went thik road agean
> His errand then wer Fanny Deane.

Here personified time is represented as a benign influence, a dispenser of good fortune to the youth. In Hardy's early verse, time is also personified, and acts in collaboration with "Chance" in bestowing fortune upon the poet—but never good fortune, as here. Hardy sees Time wearing a malignant, or at best a neutral, countenance; never a propitious one.

It is interesting to compare Hardy's *Ditty* for E. L. G. (Emma Lavinia Gifford, his first wife), written in 1870 and included in *Wessex Poems,* with Barnes's *Maid o' Newton,* whom the poet meets "by happy chance, or doom." Further than this the theme of the vagaries of chance, so often stressed by Hardy, was never developed by his forerunner.

Barnes's *Wife A-Lost* is a simple and touching lament, with an expression of the Christian's simple faith at the end. *Angels by the Door* has a slight touch of that fatalism which Hardy has always been ready to recognize as instinctive to the countryman's heart. Angels and days —Hardy's Chance and Time—bring good and evil in turn, says the poet, but there is no bitterness, but comfort rather, in the reflection:

> An' evils at their worst mid mend,
> Or even end—my Mearianne.

The very tragic theme of the seduced and forsaken woman is handled in *The Weepen Lady*. Common enough in Hardy, this motif is unusual in Barnes, who presents the poor unfortunate as cast out by her father; but, ever faithful to her child, her spirit will not forsake her old home. The conclusion is not Hardyan:

> . . . Zoo blest
> Be they that can but live in love,
> An' vind a pleace o' rest above
> Unlik' the weepen leady.

Another interesting and unusual lyric is *The Love-Child,* an expression of commiseration with the sad lot of an illegitimate child—again a fairly frequent theme with Hardy, but a very rare outburst for Barnes. He has perhaps given it even a more outspokenly passionate treatment than it might have received at Hardy's hands, especially in the glowing apostrophes of the final stanza:

The Soil (. . . 1850)

Oh! it meade me a'most teary-ey'd,
   An' I vound I a'most could ha' groan'd—
What! so winnen, an' still cast a-zide—
   What! so lovely, an' not to be own'd;
Oh! a God-gift a-treated wi' scorn,
   Oh! a child that a Squier should own;
An' to zend her away to be born!—
   Aye, to hide her where others be shown!

The humorous poems of Barnes contain no exuberance of spirits, nor violent or riotous fun, but maintain merely a fair level of geniality, as in the pleasant eclogue, the *Sly Bit o' Coorten* of John and Fanny. Hardy's humor, as we find it in the more whimsical anecdotes in *A Few Crusted Characters,* calls forth the reader's smile much more readily; occasionally it is downright uproarious.

Popular beliefs and folklore such as Hardy delighted to weave into his stories can be found in *A Witch* and in the eclogue *The Vearries.*

Blaake's House in Blackmwore is a piece that must have excited the interest of Hardy, as it presents a very palpable poetic analogy to his own first published piece of prose, *How I Built Myself a House.* It tells the story of the building of a countryman's house and of his first housewarming, in very effective, high-spirited verse, decked out with many ingenious internal rhymes.

Human nature was pictured by Barnes as being essentially good—and usually as sturdy and unflinching under the buffetings of the external world. Even in *False Friends-Like,* wherein the rustic singer announces his possession of wisdom by experience, in his distrust of the

[69]

The Life of Thomas Hardy

motives of over-friendly men (remembering a trick played upon him years ago by an older boy who invited him to ride in a barrow and then overturned him into a puddle), he retains his good humor throughout, only remarking cunningly, when offered unearned favors:

> An' then, vor all I can but wag my hat
> An' thank en, I do veel a little shy.

Even fundamentally unattractive characters like "Old Gruffmoody Grim" are regarded in a humorous and roughly tolerant manner.

These kindly Barnes-personages were not without their softening effect upon Hardy's work. William Dewy, in *Under the Greenwood Tree*, for instance, is a typical Barnes-peasant. "His was a humorous and kindly nature, not unmixed with a frequent melancholy; and he had a firm religious faith." In his poetic treatment of such themes as the love-child, however, Hardy showed himself as colder and more dispassionate than Barnes, as more calculating and as less spontaneous, although he undoubtedly felt the tragedy of the situation far more deeply. This distinction between the two poets is clearly reflected in Hardy's verse-patterns, which, in comparison with the regularity of Barnes's, strike one at first as curiously ungainly and outlandish in their rhythmic flavor. What the older poet did teach was the employment of the greatest care and the exercise of the closest attention to detail in versification. So carefully was Hardy's earliest verse worked out and perfected that he selected much of it for inclusion in his Twentieth Century volumes. Above all, it was the attitude of both

[70]

The Soil (. . . 1850)

men towards their common native district, as expressed in Barnes's very fine *Praise o' Dorset,* that formed the chief spiritual link between them.

* *

*

Barnes and Barnes's people, the ancient country life with its folklore, superstitions and language, constituted the human surface of the Wessex into which Hardy was born, and in the midst of which he lived his most impressionable years. But this was the old Wessex; it did not survive the century unchanged. Railway lines cut into the rural stretches, more devastating in their effects than the ancient Roman highways. Other impacts of latter-day scientific civilization followed in the form of machinery and factories and motor cars. And of recent years, the proud visage of Egdon Heath itself has been lacerated by the cruel manœuvres of army tanks.

Even more violent than this bitter physical etching of the landscape were the more subtle spiritual changes which have been working continuously and with increasing intensity and momentum throughout the last seventy-five years. "Enlightenment" and humanitarianism and popular education have been stamping out the antique beliefs and primitive customs of the people. Modern science and "art" have been remolding their conduct.

Formerly the church-music in the villages was discoursed by the rustic instrumental choirs, with their viols, hautboys and "serpents"—and the same choirs officiated at hilarious country dances. Now they have been supplanted—first by barrel-organs, later by wheezy reedharmoniums played by native girls who had gained their technique in the larger towns, finally by solemn pipe-instruments. To Hardy, this passing of the old and quaint spelled tragedy: Orpheus had been deposed by St. Cecilia.

The ancient weather-caster, working by divination, was supplanted by the official weather bureaux, working according to meteorological principles. An actual "skimmington" or "skimmity-ride" took place as late as 1884 in a Dorset village—but such things are now no more. Hardy himself has described to William Archer the unforgettable effect produced on him while still very young, by the sight of a man in the stocks, "sitting in the scorching sunshine, with the flies crawling over him." Today one looks in vain for a scene such as this—which may not really be a bad thing.

Varied emotions are aroused by the gradual decay of the Dorset speech, now but seldom heard. Hardy deplored it, saying:

Since Barnes's death, education in the west of England as elsewhere has gone on with its silent and inevitable effacement, reducing the speech of this country to uniformity, and obliterating every year many a fine local word. The process is always the same: The word is ridiculed by the newly-taught; it gets into disgrace; it is heard in holes and corners only; it dies; and, worst of all, it leaves no synonym. In the villages that one recognizes to be the scenes of these pastorals the poet's nouns, adjectives and idioms daily cease to be understood by the younger generation, the luxury of four demonstrative pronouns, of which Barnes was so proud, vanishes by their compression into the two of common English, and the suffix to verbs which marks continuity of action is almost everywhere shorn away.

The London and South Western Railway
Station, Dorchester.　From an aquatint by
John Everett.

The Soil (. . . 1850)

The whole situation was summed up in Hardy's recognition of the gulf that he saw widening between his generation and that of his father; between the generation of Tess and that of her mother:

Between the mother, with her fast-perishing lumber of superstitions, folk-lore, dialect and orally transmitted ballads, and the daughter, with her trained National teachings and Sixth Standard knowledge under an infinitely Revised Code, there was a gap of two hundred years as ordinarily understood. When they were together the Elizabethan and Victorian ages stood juxtaposed.

The Wessex of Hardy's spirit was the Elizabethan one, and it was firmly rooted through many even pre-Elizabethan strata. His Wessex was the Wessex of the past. His Nature, cruel and savage as She was, he preferred as She first appeared to him, largely unreconstructed by the grimy hand of man. One must attempt to penetrate the Hardy-soil something after the manner so sketchily outlined here, in order to appreciate the complication of forces which compelled the poet to indite passages like the following, from the seventh chapter of *The Woodlanders:*

They went noiselessly over mats of starry moss, rustled through interspersed tracts of leaves, skirted trunks with spreading roots, whose mossed rinds made them like hands wearing green gloves; elbowed old elms and ashes with great forks, in which stood pools of water that overflowed on rainy days, and ran down their stems in green cascades. On older trees still than these, huge lobes of fungi grew like lungs. Here, as everywhere, the Unfulfilled Intention, which makes life what it is, was as

The Life of Thomas Hardy

obvious as it could be among the depraved crowds of a city slum. The leaf was deformed, the curve was crippled, the taper was interrupted; the lichen ate the vigor of the stalk, and the ivy slowly strangled to death the promising sapling.

They dived amid beeches under which nothing grew, the younger boughs still retaining their hectic leaves, that rustled in the breeze with a sound almost metallic, like the sheet-iron foliage of the fabled Jarnvid wood. . . .

CHAPTER IV

Boyhood (1840-1856)

A Saturday afternoon in November was approaching the time of twilight, and the vast tract of unenclosed wild known as Egdon Heath embrowned itself moment by moment. Overhead the hollow stretch of whitish cloud shutting out the sky was as a tent which had the whole heath for its floor.

The heaven being spread with this pallid screen and the earth with the darkest vegetation, their meeting-line at the horizon was clearly marked. In such contrast the heath wore the appearance of an installment of night which had taken up its place before its astronomical hour was come: darkness had to a great extent arrived hereon, while day stood distinct in the sky. Looking upwards, a furze-cutter would have been inclined to continue work; looking down, he would have decided to finish his faggot and go home. The distant rims of the world and of the firmament seemed to be a division in time no less than a division in matter. The face of the heath by its mere complexion added half an hour to evening; it could in like manner retard the dawn, sadden noon, anticipate the frowning of storms scarcely generated, and intensify the opacity of a moonless midnight to a cause of shaking and dread.

In fact, precisely at this transitional point of its nightly roll into darkness the great and particular glory of the Egdon waste began, and nobody could be said to understand the heath who had not been there at such a time. It could best be felt when it could not clearly be seen, its complete effect and explanation lying in this and the succeeding hours before the next dawn: then, and only then, did it tell its true tale. The spot was, indeed, a near relation of night, and when night showed itself an apparent tendency to gravitate together could be perceived in its shades and the scene. The somber stretch of rounds and hollows seemed to rise and meet the evening gloom in pure sympathy, the heath exhaling darkness as rapidly as the heavens precipitated it. And so the obscurity in the air and the obscurity in the land closed together in a black fraternization towards which each advanced half-way.

The place became full of a watchful intentness now; for when other things sank brooding to sleep the heath appeared slowly to awake and listen. Every night its Titanic form seemed to await something; but it had waited thus, unmoved, during so many centuries, through the crises of so many things, that it could only be imagined to await one last crisis—the final overthrow.

*T*HE portentous organ-point sounded by these superb strophes, already recognized as ranking among the noblest descriptive prose pieces in our language, may with doubled fitness accompany and echo through a recital of the earliest events in Hardy's life.

Not only does it determine the mood of *The Return of the Native,* not only does it reveal the prevailing spiritual tone of the whole of the Wessex Kingdom; it also suggests the dominating character of the particular terrain which first entered the vision of the poet. For it was on the very edge of a heath like Egdon that the house in which he was born was situated. It still stands there.

Puddletown Heath and Bockhampton Heath were united to make an Egdon. And it was at Higher or Upper Bockhampton, about three miles to the north of Dorchester, that Hardy's father carried on his trade of general builder for the community. Here it was that Thomas Hardy issued forth from the womb of the Heath, of Time, and of his mother, and drew in his first breath

Boyhood (1840-1856)

of the dour Wessex atmosphere, on the second day of June, in the year 1840.

Upper Bockhampton, although within walking distance of the County Capital, stood lonely, in an utter isolation that is perhaps difficult to realize adequately today. It was a small cluster of tiny cottages, set off only by the inevitable tavern. It boasted neither church, school, nor post office. No main road ran through it; there was only what remained of an ancient Roman highway—and this seldom saw much travel. Dorchester itself, not yet tapped by railway lines, was self-contained enough, although it attracted country life a-plenty at fair and festival times. But Upper Bockhampton was virgin, untouched by the steel of industrial culture, primitive, natural—in the literal sense of the word.

The low houses, most of them thrice-ancient in years and structure, seemed a harmonious part of the landscape. Likewise the people: slow-moving, clothed in weather-worn garments whose cut, like the cut of their pronouns, had scarcely changed in generations, they melted imperceptibly into the stern and darkling countryside. The roaring life of the towns was far away, apprehended here only in vague seismographic quiverings.

The Hardy house, much roomier than the surrounding structures, was still of a piece with the lonely terrain. Emerging from it, one immediately found himself in the presence of the inscrutable, timeless personality of the Heath—a part of it, in fact, and a sharer in its moods. This inevitably remained the dominating factor in Hardy's childhood. Nothing could shield him from it completely, or for long.

[77]

The Life of Thomas Hardy

Against this effect of nature, stark naked in all its re-
pulsiveness and beauty, worked the "cultural" influence
of the mother, and not entirely in vain. The prospect of
a sheltered, gentle childhood greeted the baby Hardy,
sunned daily in a pretty flower-garden. Pleasant, amusing folktales, artificially shorn of all traces of brutality
or grotesquerie, were related to him as soon as he could
understand a tale. From the servants in the house, at
the same time, the growing infant probably heard or
overheard the same tales in their older and coarser form,
and told in the inimitable dialect which suited them so
well—delicious dialect also, its employment being pro-
scribed.

Of religion, the child likewise learned from his mother
the sweet New Testament parables and the more moral
of the Mosaic episodes. The latter attracted him more,
being more in harmony with the sad, stern music of the
Heath, which he soon learned to love more than the regi-
mented beauty of nature under botanical cultivation.
Occasionally the household journeyed in a body to Dorchester of a Sunday, to sniff the cosmopolitan air of the
town and to attend divine service at St. Peter's. Here
the boy encountered companions, of his own age and also
somewhat older, who instilled in him the seeds of that
queer pragmatic view of Scriptural authority which was
peculiar to the Wessex mind. And, inasmuch as few of
the Bockhampton Hardys were exactly notorious for
their religious orthodoxy, these seeds were permitted to
grow their heretical fruit without opposition. Still, the
Christian religion, as established by the Church of England, was there; it was to be accepted, with whatever

[78]

tiveness went a certain physical sluggishness and diffidence. The reason for this is not difficult to apprehend. The child Hardy of course associated with the youngsters of the hamlet. While he played with them in abandoned jollity, and while he talked with them in the utmost gravity, as children do, he lost himself in their somewhat loutish habits, manners and language. But when he sought to transplant these experiences into his home-life, as children do, he discovered to his astonishment that these were not the proper, dignified things for a Hardy to do. The father, and especially the mother, frowned on all that was rural or crude. Hardy learned that there was an invisible but rigid barrier between the life within his home and the life outside it. He had to learn to trim his sails in both places accordingly. At home he learned to affect his mother's manners; also, like Elizabeth-Jane, to say "stay where you are," instead of "bide where you be," "succeed" instead of "fay," "wild hyacinths" instead of "greggles," "suffering from indigestion" instead of "hag-rid." In the lanes and fields with his playmates, on the other hand, he soon learned to forget the glossy sheen of culture and polite education. Thus, at the age of six, Hardy was already leading a double life.

At the same time, the growing consciousness of his family's social position, although this position was itself rather indeterminate, induced in him a growing and uncomfortable shyness while associating with his childhood cronies. He drew himself away from them, spiritually, as his mother's attitude made itself felt more and more poignantly. He became merely observant at times when he should have been joining whole-heartedly in the diver-

Boyhood (1840-1856)

sion of the moment; he became both introspective and critical when he should have lost all consciousness of him-self in play or jest. He was forced to paint in for himself a mental background of superiority; this naturally tended to induce a sense of detachment from the "inferiority" of his fellows—and tended to constitute, in itself, a kind of complex of inferiority; for the boy was thus alone, and lonely.

It is important to realize this aspect of Hardy's child-hood, for it both determined and symbolized the mood of analytical detachment coupled with sympathetic ap-preciation and pity which was later on to characterize his whole artistic attitude. It provides a key to at least a partial understanding of his enviable mental equip-ment as a transcriber of life.

At the age of eight, the boy was registered as a pupil in the Dorchester primary school. It has already been indicated that this school was originally founded by one of his Sixteenth Century Dorset ancestors, Thomas Hardy of Melcombe Regis. Thither, at any rate, Hardy journeyed every day for a period of six years. The instruction he received was meagre enough, according to all accounts. At one time during his stay, there were no more than four pupils attending besides himself.

Of these mediocre opportunities, the youngster failed to reap any consequential advantages whatever. He turned out to be a "backward" boy, partially indolent, partially uninterested, impatient and intolerant of the extremely elementary information which the equally un-interested and harassed master attempted to impart. His mother, worried by his reluctance in progressing with sums and compositions, dusted off her old Latin grammar and began to give him regular training when he was twelve years old. Although his interests in books were somewhat quickened by this experiment, his regular school-work failed to show improvement; it remained poor, even when judged by the not too rigorous standards of mid-century Dorchester.

Instead of poring over his paradigms, the boy showed marked preference to listen to the excommunicated speech of the servants and villagers, and to those beloved reminiscences of his grandmother. In 1854 he left the school. It had given him nothing. Then Mrs. Hardy sniffed danger; she was determined, in spite of all, to civilize and to polish her son. After two years more of tutoring in the Roman writers, leavened with the reading of their more difficult passages in English verse-translations, the Hardys employed a French governess. From her the boy gathered a smattering of her tongue—perhaps also just a snatch of *l'esprit Gaulois.* For only a year, however, did this sporadic training in the accomplishments of a gentleman continue; then what has sanguinely been called the "formal education" of Hardy came to an end. It was remarkable only for its meagreness and ineffectiveness.

Jude the Obscure, that hapless boy, is thought by many to be a passionate projection of this educational phase of Hardy's early life. But even if we did not have Hardy's own word against it, this not too attractive supposition could never be held logically. Jude was depicted as eager for learning; Hardy was not. Jude perplexed and tortured himself with extremely naïve preconceptions as to the nature of the foreign languages; such things never really bothered Hardy. Poor predestinate Jude smarted under the cruel frustrations of his desires for academic and university attainments; there is nothing to show that Hardy ever overweeningly craved scholarly distinction.

Learning, wide and deep, was in time absorbed by the young poet; but it was absorbed in his own way and at his own sweet will, free from discipline and even from guidance. And, as might be expected, his learning proved to be of the vivid and thoroughgoing kind that is characteristic of the man who gathers his information and pursues his inquiries outside the walls of a university. Browning was a contemporary example of the possessor of this ample and colorful variety of erudition, skilfully applied to and permeating his artistic output, just as in the case of Hardy.

If Dorchester failed to school Hardy into respect for a supervised education, it did however present him with a unique and deeper education of an entirely different kind. He was, after all, able to write; the adolescent youths and maidens of the town were not. Consequently they fell into the habit of waylaying the young student (reputed to be so terribly erudite that he even read books in Latin and French), and of begging him to set down on paper their correspondence. Hardy complied willingly. He became the village amanuensis. The letters he wrote out from dictation in this way were undoubtedly amatory for the most part, and the authors were chiefly the girls. It was a rare opportunity for him to study the surface of human nature under the stress of emotion and circumstance, and he undoubtedly made the most of it. This education in the school of life was acquired as naturally as oxygen is acquired by breathing, and the process at first was unconscious or subconscious.

Hardy claimed to be entirely uninterested in the subject-matter which he indited; this was of course the only condition under which he could be entrusted with the precious and carefully guarded secrets of the correspondents, added to the fact that they probably considered him too young and guileless to apprehend fully the import of the glowing words he set down as they timorously whispered them into his ears. In this fond supposition they were most assuredly mistaken.

This activity again illustrates the lad's growing sympathy with the rustic heart, together with his growing critical appreciation of the machinery of the rustic mentality. Later on he beautifully capitalized these experiences of his. Reminiscential is Mother Cuxsom's remark in *The Mayor of Casterbridge:* "Love-letters? Then let's hear 'em, good soul . . . Lord, do ye mind, Richard, what fools we used to be when we were younger? Getting a schoolboy to write 'em for us; and giving him a penny, do ye mind, not to tell other folks what he'd put inside, do ye mind?"

A remnant of Hardy's actual memories of some of these epistles is preserved in a delicious bit, found in *The Hand of Ethelberta.* Tipman, Lord Mountclere's valet, is writing to Mrs. Menlove, his "intended": "His lordship impressed this upon me very strong, and familiar as a brother, and of course we obey his instructions to the letter; for I need hardly say that unless he

Hardy's Birthplace, Upper Bockhampton.
From an aquatint by John Everett.

keeps his promise to help me in setting up the shop, our nuptials cannot be consumed.''

Disillusionment of a kind, salted with humorous penetration and insight, was the great gift bestowed upon the introspective boy by this fortunate occupation. This part of his early training cannot fail to bring to mind the parallel case of Richardson, whose experience in writing model love-letters for others less gifted than himself in expressing supercharged emotions in a polite and graceful way led him to the composition of the first great English epistolary novel. Richardson, however, actually composed his perfumed screeds, while Hardy remained a mere amanuensis.

Thus Hardy passed the first sixteen years of his life: quiet, self-contained, shy, backward, aloof and generally uncomfortable when in the presence of other human beings. Drawn largely within himself, he learned to worship nature in his own peculiar fashion: to view its cosmic moods as the manifestations of an awful but indifferent Personality; to view the ferment of the same Personality in the souls and actions of men with less awe, but with added sympathy, recognizing in them the model of himself.

In 1856 his parents took thought. What were they to make of the youth? He was out of school, idle, preoccupied with himself. He had been able to cultivate but few companions. A social career was impossible, likewise was a university residence. He would inherit little or no income. Travel also was financially impracticable. To let him work with country swains of his own age, at farming or in an industry of some sort, would be fatal to the self-esteem and family pride of his mother. London was far off, and opportunities in that city extremely rare. The father's building-business was progressing fairly well, but not well enough to support another master. Ambition, besides, prompted the Hardys to discover some sort of stepping-stone for the advancement of their son.

Now in Dorchester there lived a Mr. John Hicks, an architect, who occasionally placed small contracts in Mr. Hardy's way. The two men talked things over one day. A country architect was a step above a country builder. Dorsetshire architecture was indeed more than a mere trade, yet it was not quite a profession or an art. Still, it was a convenient wedge with which to pierce the wall that stood across the path of ambition. It might, given a fair amount of luck, lead on to better things. And Hicks thought he might well use an apprentice. Many ecclesiastical commissions were coming his way, for it was said that churches all over the country were in sore need of "restoration."

Young Hardy, facile enough with his pencil, readily accepted the suggestion. He entered Hicks's draughting office at Dorchester. Papers of indenture were duly signed. The boy was launched into a career which was to provide him with experiences and opportunities as yet undreamed of. The first definite turn in his life had been taken.

* *

*

In London, meanwhile, there was buzzing a-plenty in the civilized world which awaited the young man, still unconscious alike of his powers and of his destiny. In science, religion, morals, philosophy, literature and art, in everything that spelt culture, one of the most brilliant periods in several English generations had passed its climax, was resting comfortably, and was about to slip unknowingly in decline towards the tragic, explosive overthrow that Darwin was quietly preparing for it with his patient accumulation of biological data.

The fruits of the Romantic Revolt had been reaped; a fresh consciousness of the beauties of the past, of nature and human nature unadorned, unrestrained by ugly fetters, had been gained. And the dangerous sordidness, the self-consuming flames of license that had too often accompanied the Satanic outbreaks of the opening of the century had been rigidly suppressed soon after Victoria had mounted the throne.

Wordsworth, last of the great poets of the late Renascence, had reformed, been crowned, relapsed into dulness, and died. Carlyle's barbarous, infinitely repetitious thunders had dulled many ears to the faint unrestful reverberations of the pseudo-cataclysm of 1848, that continued only in a steady and soothing *decrescendo.* Tennyson had written *In Memoriam,* Browning *Christmas Eve and Easter Day:* cogent forces on the side of an optimistic mysticism. Dickens had ceased crying out against the fantastic squalor of industrialism and was slumming in the American backwoods, to the Londoners' intense satisfaction. George Eliot had begun to ruin her splendidly human stories with moral Positivism, imported from Paris by Lewes. Thackeray was chanting of the rippling tragic comedy on the surface of the gentlemanly behavior of the time, the Brontë sisters of the comic tragedy of wild and lonely lives. Matthew Arnold was mellowing the world he saw, illusory at best, through the faintly rose-hued spectacles of academic Oxford, with its Christianized classical paganism. All these attractive forces continued to function, with ever decreasing vigor.

The glories of the Victorian compromise and self-justification were all conveniently at hand, and London was properly revelling in them. Complacent contemplation of steady, undisturbing achievement was the order of the day. That complacency had but few more years to live, for all its strength and solid building upon the seemingly substantial loam of a steady view towards a good order of things.

This London, and Thomas Hardy, diligently beginning his architectural apprenticeship, were inevitably drawing together. The Spirit of the Years was observing the slow ordering of a portentous convergence of the twain.

CHAPTER V

The Architect (1856-1863)

*J*OHN HICKS of Dorchester was, by all accounts, a rather colorless individual. A dubious fortune, nevertheless, was smiling upon him at this time. As a country architect, he could have hoped for little besides general farmhouse repair work, with now and then the job of designing a new building of a more or less standardized pattern. Chance brought him something better. It directed his efforts into ecclesiastical channels.

A veritable architectural mania was sweeping through the western counties of England. Parsons, squires and bishops were regarding their crumbling sanctuaries with dissatisfaction and alarm. The old stone and wood was slowly succumbing to the gnawing tooth of Time. Towers and floors were becoming shaky and unsafe, altar screens were fading and wearing out, churchyard monuments were tumbling over.

All this dilapidation was to be summarily "restored." Towers were to be torn down and rebuilt, altar screens were to be replaced, churchyards were to be renovated. A furious restoration-movement gripped everybody.

Unfortunately, a policy of thoroughgoing replacement was generally adopted and followed, instead of one of mere preservation of the remains of old art. Neo-Gothic styles, of a particularly atrocious variety imported directly out of Germany, were then in fashion. Down came the priceless old walls, traceries and carvings, to be replaced by hideous modern travesties of the genuine mediæval article. The mutilation of the ancient churches was terrific, brutal, heartless.

Vandalism of this kind filled Hicks's tin money-boxes and kept his staff of assistants and apprentices busy. They were dispatched out into the country, to sketch, measure and survey. Copying the designs of the old churches down to the last exact and particular detail was of course wonderful training for a young man with artistic inclinations. Hardy made the most of it. Indeed, if he had been financially independent and had had the desire and the liberty to study art when, where and how he chose, he could not have employed his time to better advantage. Many of the things he copied were shortly afterwards demolished.

Here is a picture of the young apprentice at work, as the novelist reconstructed it some years later:

The sketcher still lingered at his occupation of measuring and copying the chevroned doorway—a bold and quaint example of a transitional style of architecture, which formed the tower entrance to an English village church. . . .

He took his measurements carefully, and as if he reverenced the old workers whose trick he was endeavoring to acquire six hundred years after the original performance had ceased and the performance passed into the unseen. By means of a strip of lead called a leaden tape, which he pressed around and into the fillets and hollows with his finger and thumb, he transferred the exact contour of each moulding to his drawing, that lay on a sketching-stool a few feet distant; where were also a sketching-block, a

[90]

The Architect (1856-1863)

small T-square, a bow-pencil, and other mathematical instruments. When he had marked down the line thus fixed, he returned to the doorway to copy another as before.

Hardy lived to repent rather bitterly this ignorant and innocent sharing of his in the abominable "movement." He publicly lamented it many years later, when he addressed the General Meeting of the Society for the Protection of Ancient Buildings, on June 20, 1906. He looked back with shame and horror upon the wanton wrecking of venerable chronicles in stone, and discussed the feasibility of effecting some sort of compromise between the practical and poetically minded persons: between the users and the musers.

He told several interesting anecdotes in connection with the exposition of his reaction to the architectural practices of 1860. There were, for instance, two brothers, who returned to their native village after an absence of many years. They visited their old church, and were soon engaged in a heated argument concerning the position of the family pew—an argument terminated only by Hardy's explanation of the removal of an entire arch, upon which one of them remarked, "Then I'm drowned if I'll ever come into the paltry church again, after having such a paltry trick played upon me."

Tampering with the headstones both inside the churches and outside in the churchyards was a practice that particularly excited Hardy's indignation; and it excited his imagination, too. He told of the removal of the monumental stone from over the grave of a venerable vicar who had abjured women, and of its erection over the remains of a fashionable actor and his wife, while their stone was put in place of his. Future disinterment would make things rather awkward for the old vicar, although the actor, as Hardy remarked, would probably enjoy the situation, having been a comedian.

Continuing in a more serious vein, Hardy declared: "Unhappily it was oftenest the headstones of the poorer inhabitants—purchased and erected in many cases out of scanty means—that suffered the most in these ravages. It is scarcely necessary to particularize among the innumerable instances in which headstones have been removed from their positions, the churchyard levelled, and the stones used for paving the churchyard walks, with the result that the inscriptions have been trodden out in a few years."

The poet's emotional reaction to the same situation was dramatically expressed through a lyric included in *Poems of the Past and the Present.* It is called *The Levelled Churchyard:*

> O passenger, pray list and catch
>   Our sighs and piteous groans,
> Half stifled in this jumbled patch
>   Of wretched memorial stones!
>
> We late-lamented, resting here,
>   Are mixed to human jam,
> And each to each exclaims in fear,
>   "I know not which I am!"
>
> The wicked people have annexed
>   The verses on the good;
> A roaring drunkard sports the text
>   Teetotal Tommy should!

The Architect (1856-1863)

Where we are huddled none can trace,
    And if our names remain,
* They pave some path or p——ing place
    Where we have never lain!

Here's not a modest maiden elf
    But dreads the final Trumpet,
Lest half of her should rise herself,
    And half some local strumpet!

From restorations of Thy fane,
    From smoothings of Thy sward,
From zealous Churchmen's pick and plane
    Deliver us, O Lord! Amen!

1882.

Hardy learned to scorn the "heathen apathy" of the parsons and parishioners alike with regard to these wilful and stupid deletions of the artistic and associative treasures under their care. He derived small comfort from the reflection that some had been unwittingly preserved through the "happy accident of indifferentism in these worthies."

Here is the manner in which the novelist received the hint for his memorable scene of Jude's gilding of the Ten Commandments: "I remember once going into the stonemason's shed of a builder's yard, where, on looking around, I started to see the Creed, the Lord's Prayer, and the Ten Commandments, staring emphatically from the sides of the shed. 'Oh, yes,' said the builder, a highly respectable man, 'I took 'em as old material under my contract when I gutted St.-Michael-and-All-Angels,

---

* This line was, in 1919, amended to read: "They pave some path or porch or place."

[93]

but I put 'em here to keep out the weather: they might keep my blackguard hands serious at the same time, but they don't.' A fair lady with a past was once heard to say that she could not go to morning service at a particular church because the parson read one of the Commandments with such accusatory emphasis: whether these had been degraded to the condition of old materials and were taken down owing to kindred objections one cannot know.''

The most memorable section of the reminiscential address, and the one that showed how Hardy's intense poetic vision could be applied to the commonest and simplest of objects, was his contemning of the barbarous practice of cutting off the ''cannons'' of church bells wherever a bell-peal was remounted. ''I was passing,'' he said, ''through a churchyard where I saw standing on the grass a peal of bells just taken down from the adjacent tower and subjected to this treatment. A sight more piteous than that presented by these fine bells, standing disfigured in a row in the sunshine, like cropped criminals in a pillory, as it were ashamed of their degradation, I have never witnessed among inanimate things.''

Throughout the address, while viewing with dismay the necessity for the destruction or removal of old materials in the decaying sections of ancient buildings, Hardy insisted on the preservation of the original form and ornamentation of the structure; for, he remarked, ''This is indeed the actual process of organic nature herself, which is one of continuous substitution. She is always discarding the matter, while retaining the form.''

Nor was this particular lecture the only tribute which

The Architect (1856-1863)

Hardy paid towards the end of his life to his earliest architectural experiences. A still later memory is preserved in his famous letter of October 7, 1914, to the English press on the bombardment of the Cathedral at Rheims. After discussing the patent impossibility of an entirely adequate renewal of all the damaged portions of the edifice (inasmuch as some of them dated from the Thirteenth Century, Gothic architecture of that period being now an unpracticed art), and after deploring the losses which the window, in particular, had suffered, he went on to say:

"Moreover their antique history was a part of them, and how can that history be imparted to a renewal? When I was young, French architecture of the best period was much investigated, and selections from such traceries and mouldings as those at Rheims were delineated with the utmost accuracy, and copied by architects' pupils—myself among the rest. It seems strange, indeed, now that the curves we used to draw with such care should have been broken as ruthlessly as if they were a cast-iron railing replaceable from a mould."

*　　*

*

Hardy did not devote all his energies to his architectural work, particularly in the early years of his indentures, attractive as he discovered his technical studies of Gothic art to be. He was already inclining towards the attractions of literature, poetry in particular. The charms of his native Dorset seemed to be intensified by

The Life of Thomas Hardy

his intimate acquaintance with its landmarks, and seemed to cry for expression in meter and rhyme.

He actually composed much verse during this period, but destroyed most of it subsequently. None of it has been offered to public inspection, and only one of these poems ever saw print. This was a set of verses called *Domicilium,* an expression of the powerful effect exerted by his natural environment over his childhood and early youth. It was composed and worked over between 1857 and 1860. Twenty-five copies of it were printed in the form of a seven-page booklet on April 5, 1916, by Messrs. Eyre and Spottiswoode for Clement Shorter, and were distributed privately. The piece has been guarded with intense (and somewhat ridiculous) jealousy. Some day, perhaps, it will be possible to compare it with that beautiful section of Wordsworth's *Prelude* which was originally entitled *The Influence of Natural Objects in Calling Forth and Strengthening the Imagination in Boyhood and Early Youth.*

Tentative sketches for essays and tales were also set down by the student at this time. But when news of these ventures into a precarious and questionable field came to the ears of Mr. Hicks and the elder Mr. Hardy, the youth was informed in no uncertain terms that he was to apply himself with stern exclusiveness to architecture, under pain of the instant withdrawal of his sustenance. One may be sure that his mother had little to do with this peremptory command.

Hardy was in those days, however, an obedient boy. Besides, the threat to throw him entirely upon his own resources was something of a deterrent to unremunerative literary endeavors. He acquiesced, abandoned literature temporarily, and applied himself with more or less strictness to his official work until the end of his indentures. The discipline did him no harm, as later events amply proved. Hardy, one suspects, was never too proud of his *Domicilium*.

His tastes for learning, however, began to emerge as his unsuccessful schooldays faded into the past. With some avidity he resumed the study of Latin and began to puzzle over the Greek. The influence of the ancient Hellenic language and literature was from this time on to manifest itself in overweening measure over his work. Fortunately, he soon found in one of the young pupils of Mr. Hicks another ambitious amateur classical scholar. Together the two youths pored over their texts, assisting each other with the vocabulary, constructions and renderings. These studies, started in 1857, ceased in 1860.

Hardy had now passed his twenty-first birthday, and was rapidly learning to appreciate the value of some of the permanent artistic compensations in life: classical literature, Gothic architecture, nature reflected in English poetry.

There are hints of several important friendships formed by Hardy as he approached manhood: with a London man of letters, a temporary sojourner in Dorset, who possibly instilled in the youth his first ambition to create original literature, a person perhaps reflected in the character of Henry Knight of *A Pair of Blue Eyes;* and with a number of young men who had designs of entering the Non-Conformist clergy, and with whom Hardy

studied the New Testament in Greek while he argued
with them in behalf of the Anglican doctrines and ritual.
Possible reflections of this episode might be discovered
in the student Somerset's delicious technical defence of
Infant Baptism as recorded in *A Laodicean,* or in Jude's
attempted study of **Η ΚΑΙΝΗ ΔΙΑΘΗΚΗ.** As biographical data, however, most of this material lies too
patently in the realm of pure conjecture. For the present it must remain there, inasmuch as Hardy has evidently never seen fit to supply inquirers with a detailed
and authoritative account of any such personal influences.

*   *

*

In 1862 Hardy was at last released from his bondage
to Hicks. He left the Dorchester office and set out for
London. As a nine-year-old, he had already had a few
glimpses of the city in a rare visit there with his parents,
but he had seen little of it since. He now carried with
him an introduction to Arthur Blomfield, who held the
reputation of being a "good restorer," and a master of
the Revived Gothic. This Blomfield was at the time a
man of thirty-two, and had just achieved the dignity of
the position of President of the Architectural Association. Later he became the official architect to the Bank
of England and the designer of the law courts branch in
Fleet Street. He was knighted in 1889.

Hardy became Blomfield's assistant, receiving instruction from him in London and traveling all over the country to see that restoration work was carried out with as
little vandalism as possible.

The Architect (1856-1863)

Sir Gilbert Scott was another Gothic "expert" of the period, and Hardy enrolled himself as one of his disciples. Sir Gilbert instituted peripatetic lectures for his classes of students, conducting them through Westminster Abbey and other historical edifices of London. Scott was an enthusiast, but scarcely an expert, and certainly not an artist. Frequently his pupils showed more knowledge and discernment than he did himself; Hardy was later able to recollect, with some glee, amusing instances of such discomfitures of his Master.

With all this student-experience, it may seem strange that Hardy never achieved anything resembling success in actual architectural endeavors. As a matter of fact, he never formally completed his technical training; never set up his own office; never practiced his early profession in earnest. He never designed a house for anyone, so far as is generally known, except for himself.

At the same time, this training and these experiences were by no means wasted. All the virtues of the architectural point of view are in evidence in his literary work. Throughout his life as a writer, the mind of the architect can be discerned at work. It is almost as much in evidence near the close of his career as it is at its beginning.

Not only do architects and architecture play a large part in many of the novels and poems, but it is almost certain that Hardy's very strong feeling for form was fostered by this early preoccupation with the problems of material design. This it was, eventually, that kept *The Dynasts* from falling to pieces despite its colossal scheme and scope: and it was this that made his tiniest lyrics almost invariably assume what is felt to be their inevitable metrical forms. The novels also, despite their Shakespearean management of events in time and space, always were molded within a singularly closely knit unity of action. Their structure has frequently enough been called "architectonic." Irrelevancy in the matter of design is one fault that can never be charged against Hardy by the most hostile stretch of a critic's imagination. His early studies of architecture may not be entirely responsible for his impeccability in this most important sphere, but they undoubtedly made of him a more conscious artist in the field of literary craftsmanship than he would have been without them. From first to last his work showed an instinctive and highly developed feeling both of proportion and of decorative beauty. Beauty, that is to say, in the earlier Greek sense—a sense in which the two notions of "beauty" and "order" were conceived as identical, and in which the same word, κόσμος, was employed to express both.

The architectural atmosphere naturally served to add a large amount of its distinctive color to Hardy's work. In *Desperate Remedies,* for instance, the three principal characters are all architects. The rather colorless Owen Graye's apprenticeship at Creston may possibly have been suggested by the author's own experiences under Mr. Hicks. Æneas Manston, the architect-steward, is the first example of a rather rare type in Hardy: the almost undiluted villain. The character and the experiences of the hero, Edward Springrove, on the other hand, seem to reflect not only Hardy's earlier experiences, but even his permanent artistic opinions. There are so many

Max Gate, Hardy's home on the Wareham
Road, near Dorchester. From an aquatint
by John Everett.

The Architect (1856-1863)

points of resemblance between this earliest of heroes and what one knows about the early career of the writer, that one is sorely tempted to believe that we here have unmistakable autobiographic notes, in spite of Hardy's later assertions that an old and defunct acquaintance supplied the bases for this character. The truth seems to be that he drew partially from his own experiences, partially from those of his friend, and mingled them together with purely fictitious material to build up his protagonist.

Springrove, we learn, is the son of a commoner, but widely read and keenly appreciative of art, of a melancholy turn of mind, about twenty-six years of age, untidy in personal appearance, a Shakespeare enthusiast, and a writer of "disillusioned" verses. All of these things might have been said of Hardy in 1866.

Owen describes Springrove as follows:

"He seems a very nice fellow indeed; though of course I can hardly tell to a certainty as yet. But I think he's a very worthy fellow; there's no nonsense in him, and though he is not a public-school man he has read widely, and has a sharp appreciation of what's good in books and art. In fact, his knowledge isn't nearly so exclusive as most professional men's."

"That's a great deal to say of an architect, for of all professional men, they are, as a rule, the most professional."

"Yes; perhaps they are. This man is rather of a melancholy turn of mind, I think." . . .

"He is a man of very humble origin, it seems, who has made himself so far. I think he is the son of a farmer, or something of the kind. . . . He's about six-and-twenty, no more. . . . He is rather untidy in his waistcoat, and neckties, and hair."

"How vexing! . . . it must be to himself, poor thing."

"He's a thorough bookworm—despises the pap-and-daisy

[101]

school of verse—knows Shakespeare to the very dregs of the footnotes. Indeed he's a poet himself in a small way."

Of more interest than the rather idle question of the partial survival of the real Hardy in Springrove are the latter's opinions on architecture, art, and life, which sound remarkably like what we should expect from Hardy:

"He says that your true lover breathlessly finds himself engaged to a sweetheart, like a man who has caught something in the dark. He doesn't know whether it is a bat or a bird, and takes it to the light when he is cool to learn what it is. He looks to see if she is the right age, but right age or wrong age, he must consider her a prize. Some time later he ponders whether she is the right kind of prize for him. Right kind or wrong kind, he has called her his, and must abide by it. After a time he asks himself, 'Has she the temper, hair, and eyes I meant to have, and was firmly resolved not to do without?' He finds it all wrong, and then comes the tussle—"

"Do they marry and live happily?"

"Who? Oh, the supposed pair. I think he said—well, I really forget what he said."

"That is stupid of you," said the young lady with dismay.

"Yes."

"But he's a satirist—I don't think I care about him now."

"There you are just wrong. He is not. He is, as I believe, an impulsive fellow who has been made to pay the penalty of his rashness in some love-affair."

The sentiments here ascribed to Springrove might have been Hardy's own in his early years, but hardly the experiences with which the youthful architect-philosopher is credited. But when we recall Hardy's subsequent abandonment of architecture for verse, and of verse for fiction, particular interest is aroused by Springrove's defence of his own somewhat similar fluctuation. The following passage may throw light upon Hardy's professional artistic opinions:

"I must go away to-morrow . . . to endeavor to advance a little in my profession in London. . . . But I shan't advance."

"Why not? Architecture is a bewitching profession. They say that an architect's work is another man's play."

"Yes, but worldly advantage from an art doesn't depend upon mastering it. I used to think it did; but it doesn't. Those who get rich need have no skill at all as artists."

"What need they have?"

"A certain kind of energy which men with any fondness for art possess very seldom indeed—an earnestness in making acquaintances, and a love for using them. They give their whole attention to the art of dining out, after mastering a few rudimentary facts to serve up in conversation. . . . Then, like Cato the Censor, I shall do what I despise, to be in fashion. . . . Well, when I found all this out that I was speaking of, whatever do you think I did? From having already loved verse passionately, I went on to read it continually; then I went rhyming myself. If anything on earth ruins a man for useful occupation, and for content with reasonable success in a profession or trade, it is a habit of writing verses on emotional subjects, which had much better be left to die from want of nourishment."

"Do you write poems now?" she said.

"None. Poetical days are getting past with me, according to the usual rule. Writing rhymes is a stage people of my sort pass through, as they pass through the stage of shaving for a beard, or thinking they are ill-used, or saying there's nothing in the world worth living for."

Whether Hardy eventually gave up architecture because of similar disillusionment as to the actual relation of merit to material success, is an interesting, but not a particularly momentous question. What Springrove says of the writing of poetry is of more importance. Hardy, like Springrove, wrote many verses "on emotional subjects" in his twenty-sixth year. This was probably the most fruitful year of his "early period." It may also be true that this poetic activity "ruined him for a useful occupation." But he never passed completely through the stage of poetizing as did Springrove. The whole passage contains enough of the real truth of the matter to make it very interesting, but hardly enough, taken by itself, to form a sound basis for an estimate of the writer's real position.

Similar problems present themselves when we turn to the other novel in which architecture plays a dominating rôle. In following through the experiences of George Somerset in *A Laodicean,* from the time when he is at first encountered sketching Gothic ruins for restoration purposes, the reader is puzzled to know just where the personal recollections of the author leave off and where pure invention begins. Is the first chapter of the book to be considered as sincere criticism, autobiography, or mere fiction? It is undoubtedly all of these things, but to what proportionate degree cannot be determined. The hero is presented as a young man who takes "greater pleasure in floating in lonely currents of thought than with the general tide of opinion," who had grown enthusiastic over Palladian and Renaissance when the French-Gothic mania was at its height, who finally, quite bewildered on the question of style, concluded "that all styles were extinct, and with them all architecture as

The Architect (1856-1863)

a living art.'' Then follows this somewhat puzzling passage, which seems, however, really to represent Hardy in his own person:

Somerset was not old enough at that time to know that, in practice, art had at all times been as full of shifts and compromises as every other mundane thing; that ideal perfection was never achieved by Greek, Goth, or Hebrew Jew, and never would be; and thus he was thrown into a mood of disgust with his profession, from which mood he was only delivered by recklessly abandoning these studies and indulging in an old enthusiasm for poetical literature. For two whole years he did nothing but write verse in every conceivable metre, and on every conceivable subject, from Wordsworthian sonnets on the singing of his tea-kettle to epic fragments on the Fall of Empires. His discovery at the age of five-and-twenty that these inspired works were not jumped at by the publishers with all the eagerness they deserved, coincided in point of time with a severe hint from his father that unless he went on with his legitimate profession he might have to look elsewhere than at home for an allowance. Mr. Somerset junior then awoke to realities, became intently practical, rushed back to his dusty drawing-boards, and worked up the styles anew, with a view of regularly starting in practice on the first day of the following January.

The significance of this may perhaps be heightened by the observation that Somerset is also said to have ''suffered from the modern malady of unlimited appreciativeness as much as any living man of his age,'' and that there were ''years when poetry, theology, and the reorganization of society had seemed matters of more importance to him than a profession which should help him to a big house and income, a fair Deiopeia, and a lovely progeny.'' One must of course be extremely careful in basing conclusions on points of comparison between the rather meagrely known facts in the life of Hardy and the colorful figures and careers of his characters. But the general drift of the "architectural" sections of his works of fiction undoubtedly indicates that his fundamental theory of the absolute equality and ultimate unity of all the arts was clearly reflected in an ineradicable vein of all-embracing eclecticism.

Just as he could appreciate all styles of painting, so did he display fondness for the most violently contrasted schools of architecture. In like manner, when we follow his tastes in literature, we shall find them ranging from Gibbon and Voltaire to Newman and Matthew Arnold; from the Bible and Wordsworth to Æschylus and Swinburne.

* *

*

Keenly as Hardy realized the beauties and potential values of his architectural studies, as he walked along the streets of the metropolis during the year 1862, he felt a growing need at this time for the thorough academic training which he had never received. He accordingly cast about for some opportunity to build upon his scant knowledge of the general arts and sciences. King's College, in the University of London, happened to be offering evening classes particularly for ambitious young men who found themselves in Hardy's position. He therefore attended these classes faithfully for some time, adding materially to his mental equipment and emerging in the end with more than a fair scholarly endowment, as his later work was to demonstrate.

The Architect (1856-1863)

It was around this time also that Hardy began his wanderings through the art museums and picture galleries of the town. He rapidly acquired the invaluable ability to lose all consciousness of himself when yielding to the influence of an effective work of art. The impressions thus gained he retained in a memory startlingly photographic. He began, then, to realize that art was more than mere craftsmanship, that its ultimate value lay largely in the emotion and feeling that vitalized, as by a miracle, the product which permeated the senses of its audience.

Upon this realization, coming with the freshness and vividness of a novelty, followed a natural desire: the desire to express it in as direct a way as possible. Hardy was beginning to sense his limitations as a pencil or brush-artist, and to feel more and more distinctly the appeal of literary composition. His temperament was strongly reflective or philosophical; he was forming the habit of analysing his reactions, and of squaring them with general concepts created out of experiences and self-education. Thus he began to harbor the ambition of becoming an art-critic, and maintained this ambition for many weeks. To this end he studied intensively all the schools of sculpture and painting that he saw represented in Victorian London.

It was not until he had evolved a complete theory of art, which included the worlds of all the Muses, and until he had absorbed a vast store of useful images that had their life in these worlds, that he finally abandoned his dream of becoming an art-expositor for the press. The theories he formed in 1862, however, were destined to unify and to add vitality to all his subsequent life and work.

The most compact expression of his fundamental idea of the essential unity of all the arts was set down some five-and-twenty years later, in his poem, *The Vatican— Sala Delle Muse*:

I sat in the Muse's Hall at the mid of the day,
And it seemed to grow still, and the people to pass away,
And the chiselled shapes to combine in a haze of sun,
Till beside a Carrara column there gleamed forth One.

She looked not this nor that of those beings divine,
But each and the whole—an essence of all the Nine;
With tentative foot she neared to my halting-place,
A pensive smile on her sweet, small, marvellous face.

"Regarded so long, we render thee sad?" said she.
"Not you," sighed I, "but my own inconstancy!
I worship each and each; in the morning one,
And then, alas! another at sink of sun.

"Today my soul clasps Form; but where is my troth
Of yesternight with Tune: can one cleave to both?"
—"Be not perturbed," said she. "Though apart in fame,
As I and my sisters are one; those, too, are the same."

—"But my love goes further—to Story, and Dance, and Hymn,
The lover of all in a sun-sweep is fool to whim—
I sway like a river-weed as the ripples run!"
—"Nay, wight, thou sway'st not. These are but phases of one;

"And that one is I; and I am projected from thee,
One that out of thy brain and heart thou causest to be—
Extern to thee nothing. Grieve not, nor thyself becall,
Woo where thou wilt; and rejoice thou canst love at all!"

The Architect (1856-1863)

That Hardy's faith in the transcendent one-ness of all art was to remain more than mere theory may be shown in its application throughout his writings. He frequently invoked assistance which could be supplied only by a most intimate knowledge of painting, sculpture, architecture, music and the dance, in re-creating for his readers certain very characteristic images and ideas. For instance, in the following description of the second Avice Caro's voice in *The Well-Beloved,* the desired effect is achieved by a strange mingling of the ideas associated with music, speech and plastic art:

> The charm lay in the intervals, using that word in its musical sense. She would say a few syllables in one note, and end her sentence in a soft modulation upwards, then downwards, then into her own note again. The curve of sound was as artistic as any line of beauty ever struck by his pencil—as satisfying as the curves of her who was the World's Desire.

Since Hardy accepted whole-heartedly the notion that all of the arts should be viewed but as varying aspects of one unchanging idea, it is not at all remarkable that we find him displaying a genuine interest in them all, and a considerable practical knowledge of them as well. His point of view is very rarely that of the mere dilettante. Looking upon the art of poetry (in its more comprehensive sense—that of *Dichtung* or literary creation) as but one of many means of expressing life and thought, he never hesitated to call in the aid of any of the other arts when a suitable occasion for doing so arose. His rather eclectic early self-training gave him a comprehensive and lasting sympathy with many forms of imaginative expression.

The Life of Thomas Hardy

Throughout the Wessex novels one can find a lavish—perhaps too lavish—use of the information and terminology of the art-connoisseur. In *Desperate Remedies,* Mrs. Leat stretches out "a narrow bony hand that would have been an unparalleled delight to the pencil of Carlo Crivelli," and Manston's face is tinged with "the greenish shades of Corregio's nudes." In *Under the Greenwood Tree* the members of the Mellstock choir "advanced against the sky in flat outline which suggested some processional design on Greek or Etruscan pottery," and in *A Pair of Blue Eyes* "gaslights glared from butchers' stalls, illuminating the lumps of flesh to splotches of orange and vermilion, like the wild coloring of Turner's later pictures." One can continue through all the novels, collecting references of this kind. Thus, in *A Pair of Blue Eyes,* we find mentioned Nollekens, Holbein, Kneller, Lely, Greuze, Guido; in *Far from the Madding Crowd,* Terburg, Douw, Danby, Poussin, Ruysdael, Hobbema, and the following splendid example of art in description: "The strange, luminous semi-opacities of fine autumn afternoons and eves intensified into Rembrandt effects the few yellow sunbeams which came through the holes and divisions in the canvas, and spirited like gems of gold dust across the dusky blue atmosphere of haze pervading the tent, until they alighted in inner surfaces of cloth opposite and shone like little lamps suspended there." In *The Return of the Native* we find Dürer, Raffaello, Somerset, Perugino, Sallaert and Van Alsloot; in *Jude,* Del Sarto, Reni and Sebastiano.

Whether or not the man of letters availed himself of a

The Architect (1856-1863)

quite legitimate source of assistance in creating mental pictures by these means, and whether or not Hardy could be justified in assuming that his audiences would be possessed of a knowledge of and enthusiasm for the great achievements in the other arts equal to his own, are questions that need not be debated in a biographical sketch. It may, however, be noted that if one fully accepts the implications of the Hall of Muses poem quoted above, then one will at least sympathize and understand Hardy's procedure, even if he does not exactly enjoy it or wholly agree with it.

Of far greater importance than this practice of Hardy's is the pictorial or photographic point of view that he assumed when he created his astonishing word-pictures. This aspect of his art was perhaps given its strongest emphasis in *A Pair of Blue Eyes,* wherein one finds Endelstow House thus visualized:

> The dusk had thickened into darkness while they conversed, and the outline and surface of the mansion gradually disappeared. The windows, which had before been like black blots on a lighter expanse of wall, became illuminated, and were transfigured to squares of light on the general dark body of the night landscape as it absorbed the outlines of the edifice into its gloomy monochrome.

The attitude of the trained artist can also be observed in the picture of the singing Elfride, the changing scenes of the journey to St. Leonard's, the tremendous description of the cliff, and in the most telling glimpse of Knight and Elfie which the reader gets through the eyes of Stephen Smith. The example last named deserves quo-

The Life of Thomas Hardy

tation as a model of the employment of the painter's eye by the artificer of words:

They entered the Belvedere. In the lower part it was formed of close woodwork nailed crosswise, and had openings in the upper by way of windows.

The scratch of a striking light was heard, and a bright glow radiated from the interior of the building. The light gave birth to dancing leaf-shadows, stem-shadows, lustrous streaks, dots, sparkles, and threads of silver sheen of all imaginable variety and transcience. It awakened gnats, which flew towards it, revealed shiny gossamer threads, disturbed earthworms. Stephen gave but little attention to these phenomena, and less time. He saw in the summer-house a strongly-illuminated picture.

First, the face of his friend and preceptor, Henry Knight, between whom and himself an estrangement had arisen, not from any definite causes beyond those of absence, increasing age, and diverging sympathies.

Next, his bright particular star, Elfride. The face of Elfride was more womanly than when she had called herself his, but as clear and healthy as ever. Her plenteous twines of beautiful hair were looking much as usual, with the exception of a slight modification in their arrangement in deference to changing fashion.

Their two foreheads were close together, almost touching, and both were looking down. Elfride was holding her watch, Knight was holding the light with one hand, his left arm being round her waist. Part of the scene reached Stephen's eyes through the horizontal bars of woodwork, which crossed their forms like the ribs of a skeleton.

Knight's arm stole still further round the waist of Elfride.

"It is half-past eight," she said in a low voice, which had a peculiar music in it, seemingly born of a thrill of pleasure at the new proof that she was beloved.

The flame dwindled down, died away, and all was wrapped in a darkness to which the gloom before the illumination bore no comparison in apparent density. Stephen, shattered in spirit and sick to his heart's centre, turned away.

Hardy's use of pictorial and plastic art in his literary work is a subject that can hardly be exhausted in a short study. Any reader will be able to find almost innumerable evidences of the artist's mind behind the pencil of the story-teller and poet. For our present purpose it will suffice finally to mention two of the more striking of these instances that appear in his later work. In *The Romantic Adventures of a Milkmaid* the life of the Baron is described as "a vignette, of which the central strokes only were drawn with any distinctness, the environment shading away to a blank." And art-terminology skilfully applied to natural changes appears in this excerpt from *The Woodlanders:*

To Grace these well-known peculiarities were as an old painting restored.

Now could be beheld that change from the handsome to the curious which the features of a wood undergo at the ingress of the winter months. Angles were taking the places of curves, and reticulations of surfaces—a change constituting a sudden lapse from the ornate to the primitive on Nature's canvas, and comparable to a retrogressive step from the art of an advanced school of painting to that of the Pacific Islander.

* *

*

It is not very generally known that Hardy actually loved to dabble in drawing and painting, merely for his own amusement. Ideas which were later clothed in verse or prose frequently presented themselves to him at first as pictures, and were first set down actually as pen-and-ink or pencil drawings. A large quantity of these curious compositions gradually accumulated.

A number of them were offered to public inspection when the *Wessex Poems* first appeared, in 1898, illustrated by the author. These illustrations are striking and memorable—frequently no more than the barrenest sketches, they produce effects which sometimes become more deeply engraved in the mind than the lyrics which they illustrate.

One recalls a teeming landscape, seen shrunkenly through a huge pair of spectacles; a pair of moths, alighting upon an hour glass; a coffin being carried down a flight of steps by curious, naked, primitive Greek, male figures; a couple conversing in a Gothic cathedral, unconscious of the bone-filled vaults underneath them, shown in an architect's "elevation"; a sheeted female figure, lying on a bier; the lights of a town, blinking strangely through a pitch-black night; a Napoleonic infantryman, stalking along a hard and narrow Dorset highway, through the bleak, chilled country, a profile-sketch of Bonaparte.

Naturally these pictures do not in themselves spell greatness; they are, it is true, conceived with a preternaturally sharp vision, but executed without very much feeling for finish or for superficial effectiveness. They sometimes almost border on the ridiculous or childish, but are saved by an abiding sense of dignity, even in the grotesque. They form an illuminating commentary on the many-sidedness of an artist who was interested in a variety of things, but who forced himself to concentrate

The Architect (1856-1863)

on but a few of these interests. And when he concentrated, he achieved greatness.

* *

*

In 1863 Hardy made his greatest efforts to succeed in
the actual business of architecture. For a time he put
aside all temptations to venture into the attractive byways he was discovering at every turn, and bent steadily
over his drawing-board, his rules and compasses, his
specifications. This application soon bore fruit.

The Architectural Association for design selected one
of his efforts for particular recognition, and awarded
him the annual prize. Stimulated by this success, Hardy
prepared a technical essay to be entered in the competi-
tion for the medal and the ten-pound prize offered by the
Royal Institute of British Architects. The subject he
chose was *The Application of Coloured Bricks and Terra
Cotta to Modern Architecture.* The monograph was at
length completed, and mailed forthwith, under the sug-
gestive motto *"Tentavi quid in eo genere possem."*

The award was shortly afterwards announced. Hardy
had won the medal—but not, alas, the financial award
that usually went with it. The judge's report read as
follows:

"The author of the essay has scarcely gone sufficiently
into the subject proposed, and that portion referring to
moulded and shaped bricks has scarcely been noticed.
The essay, as far as it is written, is a very fair one, and
deserves the medal, but, for the above reason, we cannot
recommend that the supplementary sum of £10 be given
with it."

The Life of Thomas Hardy

This not uncommon manner of dealing with youthful aspirations in London was enough to nettle and discourage a young architect of more devotion, perseverance and determination than Hardy. It marked his high-water point as a designer, nevertheless. He gradually abandoned his technical studies from this time on, although he continued his jaunts over the country with Blomfield at intervals during the few succeeding years. He found himself now ready to yield to the more and more enticing siren strain of poetry—and also, perhaps, to the unruly philosophical voices of the times, which, since 1859, had been penetrating with a *crescendo*-movement into the hearts of even such self-contained lives as Hardy's. Intellectual and spiritual movements which had been blazing away over his head now began to settle upon his spirit—disturbing and arousing it more and more to the necessity of looking upon the fermenting humanity about him with increased interest and sympathy.

CHAPTER VI

FERMENT (1863-1870)

*F*OR more than a generation England had been swimming easily along through a sea of spiritual compromise, ruffled only by the solitary cries of Carlyle and the lesser Carlylites. The rising ground-swell of reform had now and again caused fears of up-heaval, but these had been astutely laid to rest by the Queen's sober statesmen. The church had been riding high and free on the Oxford Movement. Applied science was progressing along lines that might have been called satisfactory. Railways were tapping the country, news-papers were spreading information—of a kind.

It was pure science that finally shook this seemingly secure world to its foundations. The elements of revolt had all been there but had been awaiting only the snap of a mental firing-pin.

The explosion occurred in 1859, with the publication of *The Origin of Species.* Instantly the peaceful scene of mid-Victorian Britain became the setting for riotous turmoil. At Oxford, Bishop Wilberforce and Thomas Henry Huxley damned each other roundly, while women fainted under the tension. At London, an intellectual tri-angle spread confusion: the High Church corner was held by Liddon at St. Paul's; Stanley at Westminster Abbey thundered liberalism; at the Royal Institute, Huxley con-

The Life of Thomas Hardy

tinued to discourse uncompromising scientific agnosticism. The *Essays and Reviews* (innocuous reading for Twentieth Century eyes) were perused as evidence of the weakening of the religious and social fabric. The volume raised a "sandstorm" of heresy-trials, as a result of which "hell was dismissed with costs." Herbert Spencer announced the scheme of his rationalistic "synthetic philosophy"; backed by Kingsley, George Eliot and Froude, he engaged to apply a single key-conception to the whole material universe, including mankind; he saluted Darwin as the verifier of his own generalities; he attracted the bitter fire of Gladstone and of Martineau.

Thus did the Annus Mirabilis 1860 precipitate a vast unrest and disturb the placid lives of millions. With the dogmatic cosmology of the Old Testament going all to pieces, nothing seemed safe any longer. And matters did not mend. Mild people armed themselves fiercely and went out to champion their beliefs, old or new. Philosophic calm became a rare commodity. Kingsley's pragmatism ignited Newman's mysticism and created the *Apologia*. Lecky's *History of the Rise and Influence of the Spirit of Rationalism in Europe*, in 1865, followed by his *History of European Morals from Augustus to Charlemagne*, in 1869, extended the boundaries of the tournament-lists. John Morley, editing the *Fortnightly Review*, made it the organ of "fighting-rationalism"; Leslie Stephen followed in his path with the *Cornhill*. And Ruskin, who might have gone on indefinitely as an art-critic, began to look away from Turner and Venice and into the hearts of men; his *Unto This Last* led off the line of his sociological essays.

Ferment (1863-1870)

Literature, submerged in this flood of doubt and livid rage, paused irresolutely as at a cross-road. Literature, one may say, almost came to a standstill. Writers of the older order were dead or as good as dead; and the newer order had not yet found its voices. Tennyson had given his best, and now went on, beautifully embodying a lifeless chivalric ideal in the lavender verses of the *Idylls*. Browning was doing little better: "All's right with the world!" scarcely sufficed to check the world's anxious search for truth, even if unpalatable; *Rabbi Ben Ezra* and *The Ring and the Book* were merely interesting continuations of a curiously tortured optimistic reaction to tragic life; few people found themselves able to collect faith through blind energy. Arnold, ceaselessly smiting the Philistines with his polished battle-axes, aroused a larger quantity of aspiration—but his aspiration was sunk up to its chin in placidity.

It was not until 1866 that the smoldering heat of poetic revolt burst out into the liquid fire of Swinburne's first *Poems and Ballads,* to be followed in 1870 by Dante Gabriel Rossetti's Latinesque searchings for voluptuous beauty, while conventional morals withered by his wayside.

The more vigorous of the older fictional spirits were also dying out. Charlotte Brontë was dead, Thackeray died in 1863, Mrs. Gaskell two years later. Dickens, having completed his effective career with *Our Mutual Friend,* shuffled off this mortal coil in 1870. The stage was held by a troupe of second-raters: Wilkie Collins, Charles Reade, Anthony Trollope. Mrs. Craik's *John Halifax, Gentleman* was feeding the bourgeoisie with middle-class tradesmen's ethics. Against her dire influence on the public taste and morals, only two voices could be heard, both faint: George Eliot's, fading out with *Adam Bede,* and George Meredith's, just becoming audible with *The Ordeal of Richard Feverel*—both sounding in the year of the publication of *The Origin of Species.*

The decade of the Sixties, then, was a period of agitated transition; everywhere the old order was evacuating its familiar citadels with tears and imprecations; it created vacua, drew after it turbulent and unresolved novelties. England itself was changing its countenance: from a feudal, agricultural, conservative state, it was shifting into a commercial, industrial, democratic nation. And realism was displacing sentimentality in thought and art, just as geology was displacing the literal interpretation of Genesis.

*　　*

*

From 1862 until 1867 Hardy lived at No. 16, Westbourne Park Villas, in the sluggishly beating heart of Bayswater respectability. Slowly he was emerging from his architectural shell, from his artistic chrysalis, and beginning to sniff with eagerness the tainted gales set up by the chaotic movements of those spacious days. Sentimentally, he was strongly attached to the good old society that was falling to bits everywhere; but vividly and intellectually he found himself yelping with the enthusiastic youthful pack. Thus his heart and his brain were at war in his soul.

This struggle manifested itself in his growing impa-

Ferment (1863-1870)

tience with architecture and in his growing ambitions to write. He composed verses—sonnets, for the most part. In 1864 he began also to toy with prose. A little story, or more properly a narrative essay based on personal experiences, called *How I Built Myself a House,* was set down and dispatched to *Chambers's Journal.* It was accepted by the editors and appeared anonymously on March 18, 1865. It was a genial and graceful account of the troubles and pleasures experienced by a man with a small family in having a house designed and built for himself. The architect's point of view is very much in evidence, together with a rather disillusioned ground-tone,—otherwise, the piece possesses little distinction. It certainly does not foreshadow the stylist of whom Stevenson said, "I would give my right hand to be able to write like Thomas Hardy."

The spirit-searchings of the young man were fully and eloquently recorded, however, in the lyrics which he indited at this time. Many of them, fortunately, survived the vicissitudes of thirty or more years, in spite of their constant rejection by editors, and appeared, properly dated, in the series of poetic volumes which began to see publication in 1898, with the *Wessex Poems.*

In general, these extant early poems, from which, one may be sure, the chaff has been carefully winnowed out, show such a self-conscious but natural art, and are for the most part based on such a definite intellectual scheme that one may feel fairly safe in judging the majority of them as expressions of deep and lasting convictions.

Amabel is the only surviving poem of the year 1865. There is clearly traceable in it the influence of the Tennysonian tradition. It forms one of the very few links that connect Hardy with some of the aspects of Victorianism in thought and art which flourished during his youth, and of which his writing is usually so independent. In its refrain, the iterated name, "Amabel," and in its sentimentality it reminds one somewhat of Tennyson's ballad of *Oriana*. These resemblances in form and content, however, prove to be rather superficial echoes, underneath which there is discoverable a strong dash of the real Hardy. In the opening stanza, for instance,

> I marked her ruined hues,
> Her custom-straitened views,
> And asked, "Can there indwell
>   My Amabel?"

one can find the refrain and the sentimentality, but also such an uncommon verb as *indwell,* a foreshadowing of the free compounding process later used by Hardy in the word-formations of *The Dynasts,* and an "enlightened" scorn for "custom-straitened views." The lament is not, as in Tennyson, for the death of the poet's beloved, but for the dying out of the passion itself through the effects of changing circumstances and the action of "Time, the tyrant fell," although it causes the poet to wish "to creep to some housetop and weep" in typical mid-century fashion. The fourth and fifth stanzas are of interest as the first illustration of another dominant Hardy-theme:

> I mused: "Who sings the strain
> I sang ere warmth did wane?
> Who thinks its numbers spell
>   His Amabel?"

Ferment (1863-1870)

Knowing that, though Love cease
Love's race shows no decrease,
All find in dorp or dell
An Amabel.

Love is here considered as an objective force rather than a subjective emotion—as a universal phenomenon subject to certain universal laws rather than as an individual passion. The stanza is in striking harmony with one of Schopenhauer's fundamental ideas, that of the absolute subordination of the individual to the species, and with his conception of love as the mysterious working of the Immanent Will bent upon the preservation of the race. This viewpoint has little in common with the romantic or so-called "poetic" notions prevalent at the time. The young poet is colder because he sees himself no longer as isolated from the forces which drive on the external world, but as a real part of them. Likewise, in the two concluding stanzas, the usual sentimental vows of eternal fidelity give place to the logical but more disagreeable conclusions of "heartless" disillusion:

I said (the while I sighed
That love like ours had died),
"Fond things I'll no more tell
To Amabel,

"But leave her to her fate,
And fling across the gate,
'Till the Last Trump, farewell,
O Amabel!'"

[123]

The Life of Thomas Hardy

The poems of 1866 are headed by the most important
sonnet called *Hap*—a real piece of versified philosophy,
and one that sounds the distinctive tonality of all of the
author's subsequent work:

> If but some vengeful god would call to me
> From up the sky, and laugh: "Thou suffering thing,
> Know that thy sorrow is my ecstasy,
> That thy love's loss is my hate's profiting!"
>
> Then would I bear it, clench myself, and die,
> Steeled by the sense of ire unmerited;
> Half-eased in that a Powerfuller than I
> Had willed and meted me the tears I shed.
>
> But not so. How arrives it joy lies slain,
> And why unblooms the best hope ever sown?
> —Crass Casualty obstructs the sun and rain,
> And dicing Time for gladness casts a moan. . . .
>
> These purblind Doomsters had as readily strown
> Blisses about my pilgrimage as pain.

Here is the first expression of the idea of the essential
malignity of chance and circumstance, coupled with a de-
terministic tendency of thought. The great significance
of this poem lies in the remarkable fact that Hardy expressed in it a typically Schopenhauerian idea at a time
when he could not possibly have been acquainted with the
writings of this philosopher—the idea that chance and
necessity are not mutually exclusive and contradictory
terms, but that chance is the manifestation of necessity.
The failure to grasp this fundamental conception, which

Ferment (1863-1870)

is no less vital to the mental processes of Hardy than to the philosophy of Schopenhauer, is the cause of the bewilderment with which the ordinary commentator of the Hardy novels is filled at the apparently illogical simplicity with which the idea of chance is constantly introduced into a fatalistic universe, rigidly frozen in time and space. The hint of Hardy's conception of the First Principle underlying the phenomenal world as a vast, blind Impersonality and not as a personal Deity was a distinct foreshadowing of the climactic "Immanent Will" which dominates the action of *The Dynasts*. The word "unblooms" shows the characteristic use of the privative prefix, persisted in throughout his poetry, as is the expression "Casualty," used as the personification of the idea of circumstance or the conjunction of events. Time, personified and casting dice, is a natural development of the more auspicious figure already encountered in Barnes. The notion of Time as an assistant and abettor of circumstance is an idea that Hardy strongly emphasized in his early career but did not stress in the maturer poems and novels, with the possible exception of *The Woodlanders* and the title *Time's Laughingstocks*. That these abstractions are termed Doomsters is in perfect harmony with his fundamental conceptions. The poem is already so well and favorably known that it is quite superfluous to comment upon the power and conviction that speak through its telling dramatic form and expression, resulting in an artistic product of real value and beauty.

The sonnet, *In Vision I Roamed*, a cosmic adventure, calls to mind George Meredith's *Lucifer in*

Starlight, in which the poet also soars through the firmament at night. The underlying idea, and the conclusion of Hardy's poem, is far simpler, however, and is the expression of a personal feeling rather than a philosophical concept, as is the case with Meredith. The sad effects of the separation of kindred spirits on earth are diminished by the poet's enlarged vision after having penetrated in spirit "to the last chambers of the monstrous Dome." This attempted largeness of world-view marks the first step towards the all-embracing vision that conceived the Overworld-scenes of *The Dynasts*. Although he quickly returns to earth, the poet has taken his first journey into the unknown heights and depths of the universe. The sonnet is technically perfect, and contains many phrases both striking and felicitous. The expression, "ghast heights of sky," shows a handling of the adjective which is Shakespearean in its freedom, but the effect achieved fully justifies the liberty taken with the standard language.

At a Bridal, sub-titled *Nature's Indifference,* and also cast in sonnet-form, is a lover's lament for the marriage of his mistress "at the Mode's decree," a common situation in the Hardy poems. The drama, or story, although it is the "occasion" for the poem, gives way at the end to philosophical meditation on the indifference of "the Great Dame whence incarnation flows" to such a situation. Similar to this in tone are the four stanzas forming the little piece called *Postponement*. Here, however, the situation is all-important, and no abstract reflection takes place. The obvious symbolism of a bird's threnody on the fickleness of its mate is employed, and the effect is heightened through the very skilful use of the alternating refrains: "Wearily waiting" and "cheerfully mating!"

Confession to a Friend in Trouble, an adventure in psychology, is a sonnet that foreshadows the "magician in character" of the later novels in its attempt to get at a half-hidden and subtle moral and mental phenomenon. It is the expression of a vague and shamefully selfish half-thought which has visited the poet uninvited, and is a striking monument to his great and, in the end, successful struggle against a total loss of faith in human nature.

In *Revulsion,* a very fine presentation of a theme that is not very pleasing to the general reader, one can observe how early a disillusioned conception of the emotion of love had taken hold of the writer. Realizing that love is the great disturber and tormentor of man, through the agency of alluring woman, the poet shrinks from feeling its devastating power, and prays:

> So may I live no junctive law fulfilling
> And my heart's table bear no woman's name.

In this Schopenhauerian outcry against the instinct of love which brings only distress and trouble in its wake, Hardy hints at a conscious renunciation of life, with all its toil, passion, tragedy, and beauty, as being unworthy of the pain and distress encountered in living it—and this is the very essence of his early pessimism.

The tender emotion is not quite so drastically or callously treated in the series of four sonnets entitled *She, to Him,* in which the ideas and the situation are about equally important. The motif of the first is one found frequently in the poems, even in those of the twentieth

century, but is seldom encountered in the novels. It is a
lament for the fading of personal beauty and attractive-
ness while the fires of love within the heart rage on undiminished. Here also time is personified and anathema-
tized: "Sportsman Time but rears his brood to kill."
The second and third are more in the vein of pure lyric,
and express her absolute devotion and faithfulness to her
love, to whom she seems to be but a thought. In the
fourth she indulges in a malediction of her younger and
more successful rival, and is not deluded by any chimera
of unselfish renunciation, but concludes:

> Believe me, Lost One, Love is lovelier
> The more it shapes its moan in selfish-wise

—again a sentiment rather unpopular among romantic
idealists.

A characteristically ironic comment on life is found in
The Two Men. This ballad of modern life tells the story
of one man, who resolves to dedicate his life to the good
of mankind, who, in consequence, falls into poverty, gen-
erously renounces his love for her own good, and dies a
pauper. The other man schemes to live off society, also
falls into poverty, renounces his love in hopes of marry-
ing a richer woman, which intention fails, and he also
dies a pauper. So far the tale is common enough, but the
real sting comes in the concluding stanza:

> And moralists, reflecting, said,
> As "dust to dust" anon was read
> And echoed from each coffin-lid,
> "These men were like in all they did."

Ferment (1863-1870)

A very similar plot was used by Mark Twain in the short story, *Edward Mills and George Benton.* Edward Mills adopts this motto as a guide for his life: "Be pure, honest, sober, industrious, and considerate of others, and success in life is assured." His half-brother, George Benton, is dissolute, lazy, and selfish in everything, yet he wins the sympathy of his fellow-beings, including the woman who loves Mills, at every point of his career, even up to his execution for the murder of his brother, who has lived a life of unrewarded uprightness. It is interesting to compare Mark Twain and Thomas Hardy, noting how the former, beginning as a humorist and a writer of genial tales of the strenuous life of the Middle West, ended his career in a cloud of misanthropy and real pessimism, while the latter, beginning as we have seen, with gloomy but honest conclusions concerning life, somewhat similar to those of the American writer, ends with a real faith in human nature that survives his deeply rooted and early propensity to stress the theme of disillusionment and with more than a vague hint at the possibility of the ultimate rightness of things.

The Bride-Night Fire, a Wessex tradition told in ballad-form, is one of the few pieces that actually saw the light of publication before the *Wessex Poems* came out finally in 1898. It had appeared in *The Gentleman's Magazine* for November, 1875, under the title *The Fire at Tranter Sweatley's.* Like the other poems here under consideration, it was first written down in 1866. Although of no very great significance for the development of Hardy's thought, it is of considerable interest as an early humorous treatment of an incident, serious enough in itself, in the life of characteristic Wessex folk. It is also practically the only poem that shows throughout the direct influence of the work and spirit of William Barnes, both in content and in form. The entire piece is in dialect, and not the dialect encountered in the novels, but the more exact Dorset speech found in Barnes. The Barnes-tricks of more exact phonetic spellings of dialect words are also used, and footnotes give the English equivalents of all the more unusual Dorset words. The metre is regular, the quantities are always correct, the mood is always calm, and no philosophy is advanced, or even hinted at. The poem might well have been written by Barnes himself in an inspired moment, but it shows considerably more narrative power than do any of his own humorous bits of verse. This completes the poems of 1866 in the volume of *Wessex Poems*.

There is but one of this date in *Poems of the Past and Present: The Ruined Maid*, which may be regarded either as a very sympathetic or as a half-flippant treatment of its subject, depending on the emphasis,—tragic, sardonic, or naïve,—with which the final lines of each stanza—the debauched town-girl's answers to the innocent queries of her former friend from the country—are read. At the close, the country girl says to her former playmate:

> I wish I had feathers, a fine sweeping gown,
> And a delicate face, and could strut about town!—

and she gets this answer:

> My dear, a raw country girl, such as you be,
> Cannot quite expect that. You ain't ruined, (said she.)

Ferment (1863-1870)

Her Definition, written in the summer of 1866, and included in *Time's Laughingstocks,* is one of the few pure lyrics among the early poems. Here the lover finds that the simple expression "That maiden mine!" applied to his mistress means more to him than any other imaginable epithet, however extravagant. This simple and innocuous idea is expressed in a perfect sonnet. Another sonnet, written at the same time and place and included in the same collection, is *From Her in the Country,* in which the speaker vainly attempts to feel the appeal of nature, but longs for the din and distraction of the city in spite of herself. The parallel to Eustacia Vye of *The Return of the Native* is obvious.

A Young Man's Epigram on Existence, which closes *Time's Laughingstocks* may be bracketed with the sonnet on *Hap,* as it strikes the note of youthful disillusionment common to nearly all of the early verses:

> A senseless school where we must give
> Our lives, that we may learn to live!
> A dolt is he who memorizes
> Lessons that leave no time for prizes.

This bit of verse-philosophy is the last of the poems of this memorable year which were chosen for preservation. The great variety of styles and subjects, and the finish shown in their treatment, seem to indicate that these are but the scanty remains of an intense and very productive poetic activity of the young architect.

The poetical reliques of the next year (1867) are rather scanty, but include a few memorable pieces, chief among which is the curious and vivid *Neutral Tones,* expressing the remembrance of a striking but dreary landscape which reflected a very bitter moment in his life. Love is regarded as the tormentor who deceives and "wrings with wrong." It shows also the author's desire to have the mood of nature correspond always to the mood of the human situation treated.

In *Heiress and Architect* the situation is highly artificial and unreal, but the idea, the "vanity of human wishes" is strongly emphasized. All of the heiress's hopes, fancies, and enthusiasms are frowned upon and waved aside by the cold and knowing architect, experienced not only in his profession but also in the school of life, who insists on designing her mansion with a view to the requirements of the more bitter moments in life. The pattern chosen for the stanzas of this poem is a rather unusual one, but is very appropriate to the thought contained in it:

> Then said she faintly: O, contrive some way—
> Some narrow winding turret, quite mine own,
> To reach a loft where I may grieve alone!
> It is a slight thing; hence do not, I pray,
>   This last dear fancy slay!
>   Such winding ways
>   Fit not your days,
> Said he, the man of measuring eye;
> I must even fashion as the rule declares,
> To wit: Give space (since life ends unawares)
> To hale a coffined corpse adown the stairs;
>   For you will die.

*   *

*

Ferment (1863-1870)

In 1867 Hardy forsook London for Weymouth and began earnestly to practice the writing of prose as well as of verse. The two years or more which he spent at this popular south coast town, the "Budmouth" of his "Wessex," comprised a period of violently fermenting mental life. Not only did he observe objects and scenes with the eye of the trained artist, but he must have been at this time a keen diviner of hidden human motives, as they revealed themselves through the appearances and actions of the ever-varying holiday crowds that thronged the resort. Not only did he watch; one may be sure he established human contacts also. No mere amateur-student of life could have produced the many touches of psychological insight that are to be found in his earliest work. They were written by a young man who had observed and lived at the same time.

This intense and idealistic spiritual life, animated by Shelleyan visions in the midst of the gay and picturesque surroundings of the place, is probably reflected in a poem that he planned at this time: *At a Seaside Town in 1869.* Rewritten "from an old note," it was finally included in *Moments of Vision:*

> I went and stood outside myself,
> > Spelled the dark sky
> > And ship-lights nigh,
> And grumbling winds that passed thereby.

> And next inside myself I looked,
> > And there, above
> > All, shone my Love,
> That nothing matched the image of.

The Life of Thomas Hardy

Beyond myself again I ranged;
    And saw the free
    Life by the sea,
And folk indifferent to me.

O 'twas a charm to draw within
    Thereafter, where
    But she was; care
For one thing only, her, hid there!

But so it chanced, without myself
    I had to look,
    And then I took
More heed of what I had long forsook:

The boats, the sands, the esplanade,
    The laughing crowd;
    Light-hearted, loud
Greetings from some not ill-endowed;

The evening sun-lit cliffs, the talk,
    Hailings and halts,
    The keen sea-salts,
The band, the Morgenblätter Waltz.

Still, when at night I drew inside
    Forward she came,
    Sad, but the same
As when I first had known her name.

Then rose a time when, as by force,
    Outwardly wooed
    By contacts crude,
Her image in abeyance stood. . . .

Ferment (1863-1870)

At last I said: This outside life
    Shall not endure;
    I'll seek the pure
Thought-world, and bask in her allure.

Myself again I crept within,
    Scanned with keen care
    The temple where
She'd shone, but could not find her there.

I sought and sought. But O her soul
    Has not since thrown
    Upon my own
One beam! Yea, she is gone, is gone.

The romantic idealism herein reflected proved to be more than a fleeting fancy, to be toyed with and cast aside. Hardy later confessed that this train of thought haunted him for years, and supplied the motif for his last completed novel, *The Well-Beloved*.

To add color and passion to the youth's imagination came his first really important and lasting personal relationship. He met Miss Emma Lavinia Gifford, a proud, strong-willed, mentally resourceful girl, the daughter of T. Attersall Gifford and the niece of Dr. Edwin Gifford, a London archdeacon. He threw himself at this rather disdainful lady's feet, extracted half-promises from her, and under the stress of his emotion poured out a succession of memorable love-lyrics and tragic verses.

The *Ditty* to Miss Gifford (1870) has already been mentioned in connection with Barnes's *Maid o' Newton*, which may well have provided its formal inspiration. Its graceful lyric measure and its refrain produce an

The Life of Thomas Hardy

atmosphere more delightful than any of the older poet's efforts could call forth; yet the mood is a Barnes-mood, and rather free from the usual sting of the Hardy train of thought. The last stanza contains the essence of whatever pure meditation there is in the entire piece:

> And Devotion droops her glance
>   To recall
> What bond-servants of Chance
>   We are all.
> But I found her in that, going
> On my errant path, unknowing,
> I did not outskirt the spot
> That no spot on earth excels,
>   —Where she dwells!

It is a poem that does not suffer by comparison with the best of Wordsworth's "Lucy" poems, (*She Dwelt among Untrodden Ways*) though the touch of pathos is lacking.

She, at his Funeral (187—) is a striking little dramatic monologue, which illuminates a single moment in a tragedy with great vividness:

> They bear him to his resting-place—
> In slow procession sweeping by;
> I follow at a stranger's space;
> His kindred they, his sweetheart I.
> Unchanged my gown of garish dye,
> Though sable-sad is their attire;
> But they stand round with griefless eye,
> Whilst my regret consumes like fire!

At Waking (Weymouth, 1869) is likewise a dramatic monologue, cast into a rather curious stanza-form. The

Ferment (1863-1870)

theme is the transitoriness of love, the realization of which comes suddenly upon a husband at dawn, when he sees his wife as one of the common crowd, and not a prize, but a blank in life's lottery. *The Dawn After the Dance,* written in the same year and at the same place, is remarkable for its rather colloquial language, and its swinging measures, somewhat like those of *Locksley Hall,* but with the addition of ingenious internal rhymes. Disillusion is again the keynote, this time the reflection that the last year's vows of man and maid have proven "frail as filmy gossamere."

The last poem which can be definitely included in this early group is the sonnet *The Minute Before Meeting* (1871), a pure lyric, expressing the pain of lovers' past and future separation and the ecstasy of "expectance" as the time of meeting approaches. In thought and expression it seems to possess spiritual kinship with the amorous verses of the greater sonneteers of the Elizabethan epoch:

> The grey gaunt days dividing us in twain
> Seemed hopeless hills my strength must faint to climb,
> But they are gone; and now I would detain
> The few clock-beats that part us; rein back Time
>
> And live in close expectance never closed
> In change for far expectance closed at last,
> So harshly has expectance been imposed
> On my long need while these slow blank months passed.
>
> And knowing that what is now about to be
> Will all *have been* in O, so short a space!
> I read beyond it my despondency

The Life of Thomas Hardy

When more dividing months shall take its place,
Thereby denying to this hour of grace
A full-up measure of felicity.

In all these permanent remains of the poet's period of
experimentation, one can notice the complete predomi-
nance of sense over sound in the choice of words. The
language is usually that of natural common speech, used
with a freedom from mechanical restraint and with a
gift for memorable utterances. The undisturbed and
almost uncanny quiet that distinguishes his prose style
throughout, even in its tensest moments, is also felt in
these poetical efforts, giving an impression of detachment that nearly always heightens rather than dimin-
ishes the dramatic effect of the situation treated. The
principle of hard and clear utterance, adhered to by
most good poets since Robert Browning, was adopted
by Hardy very early in his career and retained by him
in times of the increasing popularity of the painted
phrase. Wherever at all possible, he used the exact
word to convey his meaning, and sometimes he manu-
factured the exact word especially for his momentary
purpose, just as Æschylus and Shakespeare had done
before him.

The most obvious example of this indulgence in freedom with the standard language, is the curious and unusual use of the prefixes "in" and "un," to signify an
absence, and not a reversal of the action, as in "unrecog-
nize" in *The Dawn After the Dance*. With regard to
this practice and to his rather arbitrary occasional manufacture of compounds, showing a general Elizabethan
sense of liberty in the treatment of word-forms, it is of

Ferment (1863-1870)

importance to note that Hardy treated the language as an essentially flexible medium, and as an instrument that had not yet become rigid and fixed. He did not recognize any established use of words and expressions which would make for a stereotyped literary product. In dealing with the general questions of language and usage in his poetical works, we are fortunate enough to possess a clear expression of his own opinion, as delivered to William Archer:

> I have no sympathy with the criticism that would treat English as a dead language—a thing crystallized at an arbitrarily selected stage of its existence, and bidden to forget that it has a past and deny that it has a future. Purism, whether in grammar or vocabulary, always means ignorance. Language was made before grammar, not grammar before language. And as for the English vocabulary, purists seem to ignore the lessons of history and common sense.

In Hardy's natural style, his colloquialism, and in his occasional use of the dramatic monologue, we can find many points of contact with the system of poetical expression adopted and developed by Browning. But with regard to situations selected for presentation, and underlying ideas and ideals, the two poets show an antipodean dissimilarity that makes any comparison an absolute impossibility.

The sonnet-form predominated in this early verse, and great skill was exhibited in its employment, both in the Italian and Shakespearean types of structure. The texture of these admirably compact examples usually carries one backwards rather than forwards in time, and reminds one strongly of the atmosphere evoked by the cycles of the greater sonneteers of the later Sixteenth

The Life of Thomas Hardy

Century in England. In addition there are encountered several very unusual stanza-forms, which seem to be original combinations with Hardy. Their general metrical regularity gives evidence of a thorough schooling in the models set for him by Tennyson and William Barnes, but one can already find traces of an aversion to the pursuit of liquidity and smoothness of versification for its own sake. Now and then the reader can detect the free displacement of accents, the syncopations, and other liberties that foreshadow the more advanced technique of his later poetry.

The situations treated in the more dramatic pieces are very seldom ideal from the romantic point of view—more often they are the more painful and disagreeable moments in love and life. This liking for sordid themes shows the point of view usually classed as "realistic," but the invariably humanly sympathetic treatment goes far to redeem the cruelty and coldness exhibited in the selection of material. There is also a curious coldness and aloofness that can be felt throughout even the more deeply conceived lyrics. The underlying poetic fervor is never found on the surface in extravagant rhetorical outbursts, but the inner force of the author's personality is only discoverable underneath the external calm of the expression.

Sincere realism in the choice and treatment of situations is an evidence of a heroic and honest search for truth, whatever it may prove to be, and a refusal to accept optimistic conclusions on any point unless supported by reasoning derived from the facts of life. If it is true that, as Emerson once said, "God offers to every mind his choice between truth and repose. Take which you please—you can never have both," then Thomas Hardy has forever forsworn the delights of repose and calm. Particularly in his earlier work, the scientific spirit of fearless inquiry which, in its psychological bearings, he applied to his literary creations, often led him to the expression of conclusions concerning the heart of man and the government of the universe that have served to brand him as the arch-pessimist of his time.

This spirit has certain resemblances to the earlier stages of Shelley's revolutionary enthusiasms, in which the doctrines of Necessity, Atheism, and Vegetarianism roughly correspond to Hardy's ideas of Time and Chance, the Unconscious Will, and Pity for all living beings. The Romantic poet, however, later showed that he had scarcely digested the iconoclastic arguments which he advanced with such fervor, and by the time he was writing *The Triumph of Life,* he had outgrown nearly all of his early and half-baked agnosticism and pessimism. Hardy's early conceptions, derived chiefly from himself, and representing a reaction to the spirit of his time rather than to a reading of exotic literatures as was the case with Shelley, kept growing with him, finding always a wider application to the life of humanity and the world, and means of expression ever increasing in beauty and force.

The extreme unpopularity of the attitude and system of ideas adhered to by Hardy might have made him the leader of a later "Satanic school" of poetry had his early verses been published soon after their writing. He can hardly be said, however, to have attempted to carry on the Byronic tradition, despite his diabolical predilections for the things that seem bizarre and shocking to the sensibilities of modern society. Nothing could be more foreign to his nature as a poet than that air of the swashbuckling poseur so skilfully and successfully assumed by Byron. His temper was very different: very rarely indeed did he throw dignity and seriousness to the winds, and sincerity was his very breath of life.

His revolt against the optimism and superficial sweetness of his age reminded Mr. Gosse of Swinburne's similar attitude, but his reaction against convention and insincerity was, if anything, exceeded by his renunciation of the sensuousness so freely indulged in by Swinburne and the "fleshly school." Note what qualities in Swinburne he singled out for particular admiration in the tribute he wrote in 1909 (*A Singer Asleep*—in *Satires of Circumstance*):

O that far morning of a summer day
When, down a terraced street whose pavements lay
Glassing the sunshine into my bent eyes,
I walked and read with a quick glad surprise
    New words, in classic guise,—

The passionate pages of his earlier years,
Fraught with hot sighs, sad laughters, kisses, tears;
Fresh-fluted notes, yet from a minstrel who
Blew them not naïvely, but as one who knew
    Full well why thus he blew.

In poetic execution, also, these two poets exhibit the greatest possible contrast, Swinburne's delight in the

mediately followed his first period of poetic activity.
One must then be very careful in applying the term "evolution" to the development of Hardy's ideas and expressions from the beginning of his career as a writer to its
close. His experiences throughout his life seem never to
have modified to any considerable degree the underlying
ideas with which he began to write. Many of the conceptions upon which the philosophy of *The Dynasts* was built
can be found to exist in embryo in his first writings,
however much they became enriched and mellowed
through the intellectual and real experiences of the
writer throughout the thirty-five years of his development as a writer and thinker. The greatest landmark of
"Hardyism" in all his work is *The Dynasts,* the really
complete and entirely mature expression of all the aspects of his art and thought. In this crowning work of
his career can best be studied the apparent inconsist-
encies as well as the things that make for unity in all
his writings. It is not of very great importance to get
the poems subsequent to 1870 dated to any degree of accuracy, inasmuch as foreshadowings of *The Dynasts* can
be found nearly everywhere in Hardy. However, by following the chronological line wherever feasible in an
analysis of both his prose and his poetry, it is possible to observe how modifying influences asserted themselves at various times, becoming assimilated into, and
enriching, his great and ever-increasing body of ideas,
and how they kept supplying new technical and artistic
aids to the poet. It is quite safe to add that if Hardy
had not in his later years come in contact with the work
of Schopenhauer, *The Dynasts* could never have assumed

Ferment (1863-1870)

its present form, largely determined by the characteristic expressions that run through its "Overworld" scenes.

The year 1870 marks Hardy's temporary abandonment of the poetic muse, and his turn to the writing of fiction, equipped with the training of an architect, the reading of an eclectic, and a full-grown philosophy of life. Already thirty years of age, he had not yet found his *métier*, but was still "feeling his way towards a method." In the period that followed he was destined to win fame as novelist, but kept up the practice of poetry just as he had done during his architectural training. When he finally, in the last twenty-five years of his life, devoted all his energies to his beloved poetic composition, he had behind him an experience and training of such breadth and depth as fall to the lot of but few men while their spirits and faculties are still at their height. His powers of observation and expression seem to have increased rather than diminished with the accumulation of years—and if his last poetry really represents the best that was ever in him, it is only another evidence of the truism that a man does best what he likes best to do.

*   *

*

Towards the end of Hardy's residence at Weymouth, the economic pinch made itself felt more and more. His poems were unsalable. Yet he had to live—and if possible, by literature. It was really necessary that he make some sort of mark in the world. Emma Gifford expected it of him. Her family possessed at least academic and ecclesiastical distinction; Hardy's, so far as could be seen, possessed none whatever. It was a case of the poor man and the lady, both extremely conscious of their relative positions.

In this emotional dilemma, the rising figure of George Meredith loomed up as a timely and useful inspiration. Meredith had also begun as a lyricist, but had as yet failed to awaken any large appreciative response. He had turned to fiction, had created Shagpat and Feverel, and was well on his way to distinction. Novel-writing, in those flat fiction days, seemed the easiest and surest route to success.

In 1869, therefore, Hardy set himself to the composition of a first novel. Into it he wrote his notions of the social structure of the times, a structure in which he personally felt himself to be rather hopelessly enmeshed. From it he rigorously excluded all lyric ecstasy.

It turned out to be a "purpose story," full of that overheated, unripe revolutionary doctrine which one learns to expect from a powerful but slowly maturing mind. Its general tone was akin to that of Shelley's notes to *Queen Mab,* which Shelley himself later saw to possess more historical than intrinsic value. Hardy's idolatry of the pure-spirited young Romantic rebel thus showed itself in another aspect.

The story, when completed, was called *The Poor Man and the Lady.* Hardy himself piquantly described it as "a kind of incoherent manuscript, which fell into the hands of John Morley and George Meredith, who both counseled me strongly *to write a novel.*" As a matter of fact, it was scarcely a real novel, being rather a crude, sentimental recounting of a complex plot of intrigue after

Weymouth, waterside and bridge. From
an aquatint by John Everett.

the then popular manner of Dickens and Wilkie Collins, added to a brave tableau of paragraphs which set themselves to mention all the things that had come under the Victorian taboo.

Hardy sent it first to Constable's, where Meredith read it and returned it promptly. Undiscouraged, Hardy forwarded it to Chapman and Hall without delay. There it was accepted for publication. Meanwhile, however, Meredith had sent for the author, and in a memorable conference advised Hardy not to publish this *Poor Man* —at least not in its original form. He urged the inclusion of still more incident and a rigid elimination of all propaganda-talk—curious advice from such a source.

The young novelist was later to recall the impression of that fruitful first interview, in the verses which he composed on the occasion of Meredith's death. They were published in *Time's Laughingstocks* under the title *G. M., 1828-1909*:

> Forty years back, when much had place
> That since has perished out of mind,
> I heard that voice and saw that face.
>
> He spoke as one afoot will wind
> A morning horn ere men awake;
> His note was trenchant, turning kind.
>
> He was of those whose wit can shake
> And riddle to the very core
> The counterfeits that Time will break. . . .
>
> Of late, when we two met once more,
> The luminous countenance and rare
> Shone just as forty years before.

The Life of Thomas Hardy

So that, when now all tongues declare
His shape unseen by his green hill,
I scarce believe he sits not there.

No matter. Further and further still
Through the world's vaporous vitiate air
His words wing on—as live words will.

Hardy had the good sense to take Meredith's advice, and accordingly withdrew and rewrote the book, adopting a gentler mode of approach for his first attempt to win public favor. But even in its revised form the story failed to please its creator, and it remains unpublished to this day. The manuscript is at present in the possession of Mrs. Hardy.

*　　*

*

Now definitely embarked on a fictional career, Hardy continued to "feel his way towards a method." He summoned his best powers and was soon completely absorbed in the first of what was destined to be known as the Wessex novels. The ambitious plan of recreating a whole geographical and spiritual Kingdom gradually materialized.

His mental equipment was of course varied and unique. Poetic passion, adequately restrained, was already his, and could be depended upon to flower into a genuinely individual narrative prose style. A philosophy based equally on experience and reading, and animated by a discerning power of insight into human characters, was to provide an intellectual framework which would unify the general impressions under development. The

Ferment (1863-1870)

setting, properly restricted in time and space, was already there, to fulfil the last of the Aristotelian requirements of the prose epic.

Finally, a broad comprehension of all the more important activities of the human mind: this must be examined in a few of its details, as it worked itself out during the quarter-century which followed.

Hardy's independent reading, for instance, was distinguished from the start for its thoroughness and depth. Take the Bible. Hardly any writer of our day has shown as close an acquaintance with the Bible as has Hardy—with both the Old and New Testaments. Not only is this shown in the great frequency of his direct quotation—a kind of pious demonstration of familiarity with the Scriptures considerably cheapened since Satan himself first showed the purposes to which it could be applied—but in many a turn of phrase that could have become ingrained into his own style only through the most enthusiastic and persistent perusal of the King James version. When Hardy was once asked his opinion on the question of the effect of the war upon literature, he referred his questioners to a passage in the Epistle to the Hebrews.

In addition to his familiarity with the Bible, he showed at times more than a slight smattering of the methods and materials of ecclesiastical argumentation. In his *Memories of Church Restoration* he related his own personal experiences with a strict Protestant bishop's objections, on purely church-doctrinal grounds, to the erection of a new rood-screen in a church in which the old one had been removed and destroyed by an ignorant builder. Likewise young George Somerset's acquaintance with the arguments and counter-arguments for infant baptism which he displays in his discussion with the aged Baptist parson in *A Laodicean* seems to reflect similar encounters on the part of Hardy with the polemic paraphernalia of modern organized religion. Here not only the Bible, but the works of the Church Fathers are handled with a fair degree of familiarity. In dealing with Hardy's attitude on religious questions as encountered in his poems and in his fiction, it will be seen that his equipment for their attack is decidedly not that of a shallow dilettante or of a superficial amateur.

His information was not acquired, nor his opinions developed, in the usual or conventional ways, with the single exception of his study of architecture. Just as his great interest in religion was plainly not fostered by his attentive listening to pious pulpit discourses from the position of an occupant of a pew in church, so was his philosophical reaction to life formed independently of any influence from intellectual books or journals. Throughout his life he seems to have observed or read nothing that would cause him to change materially the viewpoint he instinctively assumed when he began to write—or even before, although there are evidences that he gradually developed a philosophical phraseology for the expression of that viewpoint, in close relationship to the philosophy of Arthur Schopenhauer.

Of great importance to the study of his development is his interest in music, although in this field the technical terms do not flow from his pen with anything like the same frequency and ease as they do when he discusses painting and archæology. The names of composers are

Ferment (1863-1870)

seldom invoked to assist in the creation of the proper
atmosphere in descriptive passages, while those of paint-
ers are often used—with fine effect when the reader is
sufficiently acquainted with the styles of art they represent. In Hardy's work art-music is forced to give way
to folk-music, just as with many modern composers who
find greater inspiration in collecting and arranging popular folk-tunes that still survive in less cultivated and
semi-barbarous communities than in the study of classic
masterpieces.

The church organ is almost the only modern instrument for which he shows a decided liking. One of
his principal characters, Christopher Julian in *The Hand
of Ethelberta,* is an organist and composer, and reflects
the knowledge of organ-construction and organ-music
gained by Hardy during the period of his study of ecclesiastical architecture. His use of the technical terminology of music is sometimes rather bewildering to a
practical musician; yet some of the finest effects in *The
Dynasts* are secured by the invocation of music, tersely
but eloquently described for the mind's ear of the reader.
It is difficult to overestimate the importance of a poet's
acquaintance with, and love for music, and this is particularly true in the case of Hardy, not only because he,
as well as other modern poets, sometimes imitated in his
verse the free and natural rhythms of modern music, but
also because he has so often been accused of indulging in
a total disregard for melody, fluency, and general beauty
of sound in his poetry.

Finally, his wide knowledge and great skill in the technique of both metrical and narrative form was picked

up and highly developed by him without any outside assistance worth mentioning. Largely self-educated in literature, art, and science, he showed at times the small and characteristic defects of training usual to those who have been thrown back upon their own resources for a higher education; but these faults were greatly outweighed by the advantages which such conditions usually prove to present to ardent and creative spirits: an imperishable interest in knowledge for its own sake, and a continually fresh desire for the investigation of anything and everything that seems to possess beauty or utility— a desire that was never dulled or oversatiated by the blight of the rigid enforcement of the uncongenial academic point of view.

It is not surprising to find that his tastes ran to Greek tragedy, with which his own work has been compared more often, perhaps than has that of any other modern English author. Of the three great tragic writers of Athens, he showed a marked preference for the earliest and most austere, Æschylus. It is perhaps remarkable that he did not develop a greater enthusiasm for the more unorthodox and revolutionary Euripides, but he must have felt a closer kinship between himself and the oldest member of the illustrious triumvirate, preoccupied as the latter was with the problems of Destiny and the justification of the ways of Providence to man. There is also a decided affinity of poetical style between the two, both having been much criticised by their contemporaries for their harshness, obscurity, and general unconventionality of language. Among Latin authors Hardy found no such heroes or models, although now and then he betrayed an interest in Horace, whose lyrical odes were certainly models for many of his early poems, it being doubtful whether his erudition had extended so far as to include a reading of the Æolic dialect of the Sapphic fragments or of Alcæus.

The smattering of French picked up from his governess was improved upon by his study in the evening classes at King's College. His knowledge of the language does not seem to have led him to investigate the literature of France very carefully, however. Except for a few scattered expressions, the quotation of the French source of his poem *The Peasant's Confession,* and a popular Parisian ditty sung by Clym in *The Return of the Native,* no Gallic influence is traceable in his work. His interpretation of "the French character" he presented in what he termed the "romantic" figures of Francis Troy in *Far from the Madding Crowd,* of Damon Wildeve in *The Return of the Native,* and of Felice Charmond in *The Woodlanders.* His German was picked up while he was engaged upon the writing of fiction, as is shown by the increasing number of allusions to the literature of that language in the later novels. Goethe alone of the poets seems to have attracted him, although the idealistic philosophers greatly fascinated him towards the end of the fiction-episode in his career.

The entire field of English lyrical poetry was familiar ground to him. His third novel, *A Pair of Blue Eyes,* contains chapter-mottoes drawn from more or less familiar poems ranging from the Earl of Surrey to Tennyson. In his last published novel, *The Well-Beloved,* the sections are headed by lyrics from Crashaw, Wyatt, and

[153]

Shakespeare. His comparative indifference to the Euripidean pity for humanity and spirit of revolt was atoned for in his intense admiration for Shelley, more frequently quoted in his writings than any other single poet. His attachment to the youthful and tragic figure of the "master of those that sing" has a certain significance apart from the purely literary influence of the earlier poet on the later. The two temperaments show striking affinities.

*   *

*

With this apparatus at hand, Hardy began to perform the most effective and successful tasks of his career. It will be interesting to observe later how his equipment was enlarged and polished by the time he was approaching the turn of the century and returning to the abandoned embraces of his lyric muse. But meanwhile, there are events of importance to relate.

CHAPTER VII

The Novelist (1870-1898)

*S*TILL remembering Meredith's admonition: "Less talk—more incident!" Hardy finished *Desperate Remedies* late in 1870. It was a tale of mystery, sensation, murder, conflagration, attempted rapine and miscellaneous thrills, artificial and unconvincing, relieved only by a few scenes from rural life, such as the cider-pressing episode. There was some difficulty about having it printed, but the author finally discovered that "Old Tinsley" of Tinsley Brothers would undertake its publication, provided that Hardy himself would agree to endow the work with an advance payment of £75. A record of this interesting transaction is contained in Hardy's letter to Tinsley, written from Bockhampton on December 20th.

Tinsley has been rather unfairly abused for his insistence on such a financial arrangement. It should be remembered that Hardy at this time, although over thirty years of age, had really very little evidence at hand to demonstrate his powers as a writer of prose. He himself did not acknowledge the novel. It appeared anonymously, and to all later editions he attached a very apologetic preface, making it apparent that he did not wish the book to be taken too seriously. Tinsley's conduct was further justified by the reception—lack of reception, rather—accorded the work.

It attracted no notice whatever, and remained almost totally unknown until it was revived by the growing interest in Hardy's maturer work. It was practically inaccessible to English readers until the appearance of its second edition eighteen years later, although it had been reprinted in America. Copies of the three-volume first edition are to-day extremely rare.

Meredith again was interested in the rather dynamic, if crudely developed, "drive" of the narrative. He certainly had no further cause for complaint on the score of paucity of incident and plot. In another interview with Hardy he advised a lightening and brightening of tone-color.

This advice again took immediate effect. It resulted in the most pleasing idyl among all the Wessex novels, *Under the Greenwood Tree,* written after Hardy had definitely forsaken Weymouth and had returned to the inland villages of Dorset, where he could again feel himself to be the countryman born and bred. The full flavor of the countryside can be sensed in this story. It remains the most popular of the series, with the possible exception of *Tess,* probably because it is the least painful in its effects upon sensitive readers. It was greatly admired by both Tennyson and Browning. Its lightly sketched-in undertone of irony, which casts dun shadows over the concluding paragraphs particularly, went largely unnoticed.

From September, 1872, to July, 1873, *Tinsley's Magazine* ran a serial story called *A Winning Tongue Had He.* This narrative was then issued in three volumes, again by Tinsley Brothers, under the revised title, *A Pair of*

The Novelist (1870-1898)

Blue Eyes. Both historically and intrinsically, this novel is one of the most important of the series. It was the first book that Hardy acknowledged as his own from the start, and for its plot, melodramatic thrills, characterization, nature-machinery, acid irony and occasional gentleness and humor, may fairly be called the first really characteristic Hardy-novel. Its reception was not enthusiastic.

Ample atonement for all this public and critical apathy was accorded, however, in the greeting which was bestowed upon *Far from the Madding Crowd,* which began to run anonymously in the *Cornhill Magazine* in 1873, and which was published in two volumes by Smith, Elder & Co. in 1874. There was much speculation as to its authorship. Strangely enough, it was thought by many to be a late work of George Eliot, who had long since passed the *Silas Marner* and *Mill on the Floss* stage of her career. The Wessex folk in the tale drew much unfavorable comment, however; one reviewer characterizing the inimitable Joseph Poorgrass as a "preëminent bore." Edmund Gosse remembers that the dialect of the rustics was also called "odd scraps of a kind of rural euphuism . . . a queer mixture, very dreary and depressing."

In spite of these and similar blunders on the part of readers, the book achieved an instant and considerable vogue. Encouraged by this first material success, Hardy and Miss Gifford decided to risk matrimony. They were quietly married, and immediately established themselves in Dorset, first at Stourminster-Newton, the "Stourcastle" of the novels. Then they removed to London, where they lived, off and on, for several years, and later to

The Life of Thomas Hardy

Wimborne. Here the Hardys resided, with frequent absences in London and in a Paris flat near the Quai Voltaire, until they moved into their present home, Max Gate.

Instead of immediately and whole-heartedly following up *Far from the Madding Crowd* with another effort in similar vein, the "coming" novelist felt at this time a strong iteration of the impulse to devote his entire energy to composition in verse. But he was persuaded by Leslie Stephen to continue with his novels, particularly with *The Return of the Native,* which he had had in hand for some years. From 1870 to 1874 he had produced an important book each year, but there followed an interval of four years before the actual completion and publication of his prose epic of Egdon Heath.

Meanwhile, in 1876, *The Hand of Ethelberta,* a "comedy in chapters . . . a somewhat frivolous narrative," as he called it, had appeared, and had added little to his reputation, although it is a unique work, and of considerable importance for the study of the development of his art. His preface to the edition of 1895 presented the book as an argument for social liberalism in comedy, defending the claims of the servants' hall as a proper scene for artistic drama.

In these unhurried years of his career, Hardy continued to write poetry—verse remained throughout his favorite means of literary expression. His ambition to become a great poet was never submerged under a sense of his undoubted success, in spite of himself, as a novelist. It was hinted again and again that only the necessity for earning a livelihood kept him writing fiction.

The Novelist (1870-1898)

Leslie Stephen at this time exercised other influences over Hardy besides keeping him at his novels. The conversation of the two men, in London and in Dorset, was reported by Edmund Gosse to have "obstinately turned upon theologies decayed and defunct, the origin of things, the constitution of matter, and the unreality of time." Of such metaphysics in the stricter sense, however, one can find but few remaining traces until one looks at the supernatural machinery of *The Dynasts* and some of the later lyrical poems. All the evidence at hand seems to indicate that the consistent philosophy at the base of all of Hardy's output was less the result of erudition than the effect of the peculiar characteristics of his very individual personal temperament.

With the publication of *The Return of the Native* began the long series of controversies on modern art and morals which followed nearly every one of his subsequent works. "I recollect the zeal with which the late Bishop of London, Mandell Creighton, scandalized a company at his own dinner-table by what seemed then an absolutely extravagant laudation of it," wrote Gosse in 1901.

Nevertheless, popularity came but laggingly to Hardy. It is related that he once accompanied Rudyard Kipling on a search for a seaside cottage, to be shared by both authors during the summer months. They found a suitable house in the neighborhood of Weymouth, and proceeded to negotiate for its rental. Unawed by Hardy's then imposing full beard, the landlady demanded references.

"Why," said Hardy, "this is Mr. Kipling."

The Life of Thomas Hardy

"Mr. Kipling? . . ."

"Rudyard Kipling, the famous Indian balladist."

"Rudyard Kipling? . . ."

The woman had never heard of him, so Kipling himself carried on:

"But this is Mr. Hardy."

"Mr. Hardy? . . ."

"Thomas Hardy, the great Wessex novelist."

"Thomas Hardy . . . Wessex? . . ."

She had never heard of either of them. This happened in the present century. Such is the fame of even successful littérateurs.

The record for Hardy's next two decades can be little more than an annotated catalogue:

1880: *The Trumpet-Major,* the most genial of the novels; the first evidence of the growing hold which the Napoleonic legend was assuming over the author.

1881: *A Laodicean,* dictated through a wearisome illness of six months, to a predetermined happy ending, featuring architecture, designed to appeal to less mature readers, particularly youngsters into whose souls the iron had not yet entered.

1882: *Two on a Tower;* the lonely lives of a boy-astronomer and an indiscreet lady of quality, projected against a stellar background.

1886: *The Mayor of Casterbridge,* the profound effect of Biblical influences—a simple, headstrong character, relentlessly pursued to his doom by a Nemesis at once drawn out of the Old Testament and Greek tragedy.

1887: *The Woodlanders,* German idealistic philosophy,

Thomas Hardy in 1890. From a photograph published in *The Pall Mall Budget*.

The Novelist (1870-1898)

a dramatic metaphysical flame, illuminating a tale of virginal passion.

1888: *Wessex Tales,* novelettes, masterpieces of short-story technique.

1891: *A Group of Noble Dames,* local heroines, tragic and comic, fitted into a Chaucerian framework.

1891: *Tess of the D'Urbervilles,* the sensational tragedy of the virtuous seduced woman. *Tess* was the fruit of many months of reflection and research. There is an anecdote which explains how much of Hardy's material was acquired, and throws a little light on the character of his first wife. The originals for the famous D'Urberville portraits were actually hanging in the manor house at Wool. The Hardys called there in order to obtain a view of them. Admission was denied, however, and they were turning away in disappointment, when Mrs. Hardy fell in a faint. She refused to revive until they had carried her into the house. Her husband naturally accompanied her within. Thus the pictures were viewed. Copies were subsequently painted for Hardy by John Everett.

Upon the publication of *Tess,* the discussion of the ethical implications and moral values of Hardy's "message" reached feverish intensity, and finally assured him of large sales. *Tess* remains his best seller; it has even been filmed.

1894: *Life's Little Ironies,* the best of the collections of briefer stories; the most tragical and the most comical juxtaposed in *A Few Crusted Characters.*

1895: *Jude the Obscure,* the story of the male counter-

The Life of Thomas Hardy

part of *Tess*, a still more passionate study of unusual psychological phenomena of an erotic type, aggravated by their setting in conditions governed by characteristically British social and academic prejudices. A copy of this "dangerous" book was publicly incinerated by an official of the Church, possibly, as Hardy remarked, because of his chagrin at being unable to accord the same treatment to its author.

1897: *The Well-Beloved,* a curious, semi-allegorical, semi-absurd treatment of the vagaries of ideal love.

In 1913 the scattered remains of Hardy's fiction were gathered together in a single volume, called *A Changed Man and Other Stories.* These, together with the stray essays recently collected and published under the title *Life and Art,** complete the sum of his significant prose works.

*   *

*

Max Gate was built in 1885, from Hardy's own designs, not far from the house of William Barnes. By a turn of circumstance worthy of a place in the novels, the tract of land selected for the site of his permanent home was found to cover an ancient Roman cemetery, containing the remains of a whole platoon of Hadrian's military forces, and of a lady of evident nobility, whose brooch is now an interesting item in Hardy's collection of local antiquities.

*   *

*

---

* Greenberg, Inc., New York, 1925.

The Novelist (1870-1898)

Most of us still regard Hardy merely as a novelist and nothing more, and hence consider the books that he wrote between 1870 and 1895 as his chief claim to distinction. Hardy himself has always disagreed with this probably premature judgment. He himself regarded these twenty-five years as a mere preparation for the tasks which he really wished eventually to accomplish.

The way was now cleared. He was known as a successful, vital writer. His livelihood was assured; he was "fixed"—alas, too "fixed," perhaps, in the popular mind.

At any rate, he now approached another turning-point in his career. He contemplated the final abandonment of prose and the utter dedication of his powers to the service of the poetic muse. It would be idle to deny that the writing of the Wessex novels had not fitted him eminently for his subsequent rhyming. In 1869 his equipment had been broad, but sketchy; by 1897 his knowledge and appreciation of most of those artistic adjuncts which make the effective poet had ripened, deepened and increased immeasurably in intensity.

When we consider the art of music, a subject of the highest importance for the modern poet, we find Hardy paying eloquent tributes to its power and soul-stirring beauty. Testimony that he did not rank music among the least of the arts, in spite of what has sometimes been said about the "unmusical" quality of his verse, is not wanting in his prose writings, although it will be seen that he gave more attention to certain kinds of rural and folk-music than to the more highly developed art-music of the cultural centres.

The Life of Thomas Hardy

One of the memorable scenes in *Desperate Remedies* is that of Manston's playing of his organ to Cytherea, in which the influence of the powerful strains of music as produced by his practical hand are represented as shaking and bending the impressionable girl "as a gushing brook shakes and bends a shadow cast across its surface." In contrast to the rather sinister spell exercised by the art here, one might call attention to the wonderful power for good which the strains of the hymn, "Lead, Kindly Light," have over the tortured soul of Bathsheba in *Far from the Madding Crowd*. Tess's innate love of melody, also, "gave the simplest music a power over her which could well-nigh drag her heart out of her bosom at times."

Hardy's knowledge of the history and of the technical side of the art may not have been as great as his knowledge of painting, but he could at times make telling use of the information he possessed. Thus the elm-tree with which John South's life is bound up, gives forth melancholy "Gregorian melodies," Eustacia's presence calls to mind Mendelssohn's march in "Athalia," and Mop Ollamoor might have been "a second Paganini." The Baptists in *A Laodicean* sing a rather long hymn "in minims and semibreves," and the Trumpet Major possesses the faculty of "absolute pitch." In *The Mayor of Casterbridge* the sounds emanating from Ten-Hatcher-Wier are likened to the various voices of a symphony orchestra.

Christopher Julian in *The Hand of Ethelberta* is the only professional musician who plays a major part in any of the novels. He belongs to the variety known as "organist-composers," and, as an all-around musician, proves a suitable vehicle for Hardy's opinions on the profession. Of his circumstances we learn that in comparison with starving, he thrived; "though the wealthy might possibly have said that in comparison with thriving he starved." Ethelberta's musicale provides a beautiful opportunity for criticism of the usual attitude of the cultured public towards the cultivated art they profess to admire.

Not only the unappreciative public, but the creative musician himself, when he loses sight of his ideals in his efforts towards material advancement, called forth most satiric comment from Hardy. Jude the Obscure, stirred to his soul by the strains of the hymn, "The Foot of the Cross," imagines its composer as one who would, of all men, understand his difficulties. The interview that he finally obtains is one of the great disillusionments of his life. In place of the full and throbbing soul he had thought to find, he meets a respectable, but shabby-genteel, and altogether mercenary spirit.

Although one may come across references to a great variety of musical subjects in the stories, including the ever-popular arts of singing, piano-playing, and the like, Hardy's preferences usually run to phases of musical expression that do not generally appear in metropolitan concert-halls. His interests lie rather in such things as the efforts of a humble shepherd with the flute he loves, in a soldier's affection for his martial trumpet, in that curious and almost extinct instrument, the serpent, or

"Schlangenrohr," and in a crudely constructed æolian harp, the mournful notes of which are fraught with suggestion.

The only modern concert-instrument for which Hardy seems to have a decided liking is the organ. His experience as a church-architect is probably largely responsible for his intimate acquaintance with its parts and with the effects that it can produce. He likens the wooden tones of the wheels and cogs of the flour-mill to the distinctive quality of the stopped diapason pipes of an organ; the mournful wind sounding through the chimney reminds him of its deep and hollow pedal tones; and a sensitive woman's quivering lip is to him like a tremolo-stop opened in her speech. With regard to organ-performers, we notice that in addition to Jude, the poorly equipped amateur, Manston, the well-trained amateur, and Christopher Julian, the professional, there is another most interesting "semi-professional" class, represented by Fancy Day, Elfride Swancourt, and Tabitha Lark. These rural young ladies figure as the supplanters of the ancient local string-choirs, of which Hardy was so enamoured.

Religious music, in general, was employed by him in preference to other kinds, for incidental use in heightening the effects he wished to achieve. That he had at least some knowledge of the history of church-music in England is shown by Somerset's ruminations over the tune "The New Sabbath," in the first chapter of *A Laodicean*. He recollects that the tune appertained to the old west-gallery period of church-music, anterior to the great choral reformation and rule of Monk—that old time when

The Novelist (1870-1898)

the repetition of a word, or half-line of verse, was not considered a disgrace to an ecclesiastical choir. The old psalm-tunes, familiar and dear to every true Englishman's heart, often add a wealth of suggestion to incidents and situations. As an inn burns down to the ground, the bewildered chimes of the near-by church "wander through the wayward air of the Old Hundred and Thirteenth" and when the unfortunate Cytherea has been deserted by her Edward, the well-known verses of the First, cause "that sphere-descended maid, Music, friend of Pleasure at other times," to become a positive enemy—racking, bewildering, unrelenting. Turning for illustrations from the earliest novel to the latest, a remarkable passage from *Jude the Obscure* might be mentioned as an instance of the dramatic use of church-music. It will be remembered that the repentant Jude enters the Cathedral-Church of Cardinal College at Christminster just as the choir intones the second part, *In quo corriget,* of the 119th Psalm, stirred by the question, "Wherewith shall a young man cleanse his way?" A more tragic and a stupendously ironic effect is achieved by the same means later on. After Little Father Time's hanging of himself and of the children of Sue and Jude, the two miserable parents are aroused from the stupor that had succeeded their first shock of horror by the notes of the organ of the College chapel. Jude recognizes the music as the anthem from the Seventy-third Psalm: "Truly God is loving unto Israel."

The substitution of the single organist for the string-choir in rural communities is a theme that runs through much of Hardy's work, but finds its most complete expression in *Under the Greenwood Tree*. He loved to think of the old bands of musicians, with their quaint and naïve ways, and the beautiful effects achieved by their noels on Christmas-eve. His heart went out to them for their earnestness and zeal in the performance of their tasks, which they did as a real labor of love; and their passing away before the advance of the tastes of "fashionable society" filled him with sadness. His treatment of the old instrumentalists and singers of Mellstock, Longpuddle, and other localities, is not always melancholy or serious,—they provided him at times with material for the most delightfully humorous passages in his works. The curious juxtaposition of religious and profane matter in their music-books calls forth some rather sprightly comment, and the anecdote entitled *Absent-mindedness in a Parish Choir* shows Hardy in his very gayest mood. It is really uproariously funny.

Popular and folk-music always possessed great attractions for him. He used "The Break o' the Day" and other ditties that were supposed to induce the cows to let down their milk, in *Tess,* and Donald Farfrae enraptures his audience in "The Golden Crown" with his singing of the emotional Scotch folk-melodies.

Closely allied to Hardy's treatment of music are his references to, and his employment of, the art of the dance. The village choirs, of which he was so fond, play not only psalms, but officiate on festive occasions with the livelier sections of their repertoires. The psychological effect of the crescendo of excitement as produced by the country-dances with which he was familiar, often plays a large part in the development of his stories. The

The Novelist (1870-1898)

dance at the "gypsying" in *The Return of the Native,* for instance, is conceived as one of the most powerful influences that attract Eustacia and Wildeve to each other, and to their own destruction. It is at Paula's first dance that Somerset discovers his affection for her, and it is by his reckless dancing at Etretat that he draws her to him, repentant. The excitement of the dance leads the two Hardcome cousins to exchange life-partners on the eve of their weddings, which rash decisions bring on their inevitable tragic consequences. Mop Ollamoor steals back his child by forcing the unfortunate Carline to dance herself to exhaustion under the influence of the seductive strains of his fiddle. Dancing, even in its more refined forms, was viewed by Hardy less as an esthetic phenomenon, or as an art in the stricter sense, than as a purely physio-psychological phenomenon which carries with it certain ethical considerations.

Before attempting to distill from his writings Hardy's ideas on the function and practice of the art of poetry itself, it might be well to observe the actual extent of his acquaintance with the literature of all times, with the aim of discovering his qualifications as a critic of his own chosen art. In the first place, it will be noticed that he displayed a remarkable, it might almost be said, a phenomenal, familiarity with that fountain-head of forcible and beautiful expression, the Bible. His books are full, not only of quotations from the King James Version, but of innumerable less tangible echoes of the fine old Biblical phraseology—turns of phrase that might have been conceived by the Psalmist. In his very first novel, the references run practically all through the Old Testa-

The Life of Thomas Hardy

ment: the stories of Adam, Abraham, Joseph and Pharaoh, Samuel and Elijah, are alluded to, and the reader is already made aware of his fondness for the Psalms. In *A Pair of Blue Eyes,* one comes across Judges, Kings, Ruth, Isaiah, and many other books, of both the Old and the New Testament, and the rhymed Psalter figures again. One might continue to gather such references throughout Hardy's writings. That his language, and, to some extent, his very mode of thought, is saturated with Scriptural flavor, few who read his books can deny. It is perhaps in *The Book of Job* that he finds most food for his enthusiasm—at any rate the immortal words that he puts into the mouth of the dying Jude, punctuated by the "hurrah's" of the gay crowd outside the house, stir the soul of the reader as nothing else could. The words of King Lemuel in the Proverbs, beginning, "Who can find a virtuous woman?" are used with a remarkable ironical effect in *Tess,* and in *The Mayor of Casterbridge,* Henchard's compulsion of the village choir to play the tune of the savage 109th Psalm represents the author's belief in the truth to life of Old Testament doctrines, and his criticism of them, on moral grounds. This seems to indicate that although he probably had no knowledge of Hebrew, he was acquainted with the general trend of Biblical criticism.

With the New Testament Hardy is even more familiar than with the Law and the Prophets. The title of one of his novels was taken from the Revelation. Certain passages in *Jude the Obscure* and in *A Tragedy of Two Ambitions* seem to show that he had some acquaintance with the Greek original. Sue Bridehead not only indulges in the usual kind of criticism to which the *Song of Solomon* and its chapter-headings are usually treated, but also advocates the printing of the books of the New Testament in the order in which she conceives them to have been written, beginning with *Romans,* and putting the gospels much further on. Hardy is familiar not only with the books in the generally accepted canon of both Testaments, but also with the Apocrypha. Thus, one of the divisions of *Jude* is headed by an excerpt from the apocryphal Esther, and the rejected books of the New Testament, notably the Gospel of Nicodemus, are discussed by Sue. Even extra-Biblical religious literature, from the writings of the Church Fathers to those of Jeremy Taylor, Butler, Doddridge, Pusey, and Newman, must at some time or other have attracted his interest and attention.

It has often been pointed out that Hardy's work has much in common with that of the more austere of the ancient classical writers. Without following out the important and interesting analogies that suggest themselves in this connection, it might be well to discover first the actual extent of his acquaintance with the Greek and Latin languages and literatures. Although he was trained in Latin early in life, he picked up his Greek chiefly by his own efforts. At any rate, he displays a considerable first-hand knowledge of Greek, especially Greek tragedy, and, what is more uncommon, a genuine interest in it as well. Æschylus in particular exerted a permanent influence over his work; and this in spite of his

The Life of Thomas Hardy

repeated denials of any real intellectual affinity between himself and the ancients, and his occasional misunderstanding of the classical authors to whom he alludes.

The casual references to Greek literature range from Homer, Sappho, Hippocrates and Sophocles, to Menander, Plato, Diogenes, Laertius, and Eudoxus, the astronomer, but the most numerous and the most striking direct uses of the remains of ancient writings are found in his employment of phraseology and of complete excerpts from Æschylus the tragedian. The intensely ironic close of *Tess of the D'Urbervilles* is of course the first instance to come to mind: " 'Justice' was done, and the President of the Immortals (in Æschylean phrase) * had ended his sport with Tess." Of equal significance is the reference found in the most tragic section of *Jude the Obscure*:

"I am a pitiable creature," she said, "good neither for earth nor heaven any more! I am driven out of my mind by things! What ought to be done? She stared at Jude, and tightly held his hand. "Nothing can be done," he replied. "Things are as they are and will be brought to their destined issue." She paused. "Yes! Who said that?" she asked, heavily. "It comes in the chorus of the *Agamemnon*. It has been in my mind continually since this happened."

W. S. Durrant has also called attention to the strong "atmospheric" effect produced by Sue's comment upon the tragic story of the Fawleys' ancestor who was gibbeted near the Brown House: "It makes me feel as if a tragic doom overhung our family as it did the House of

---

*πρύτανις μακάρων, Æsch. Prom.

The Novelist (1870-1898)

Atreus." Even in a discussion of realism in literature Hardy was inevitably reminded of Æschylus's masterpiece, when he wrote, "All really true literature directly or indirectly sounds as its refrain the words in the *Agamemnon:* 'Chant Ælinon, Ælinon! But may the good prevail.'"

With Latin he was fairly familiar, but not more so than the average educated Englishman. In his earliest book he quoted, somewhat pedantically, from the Latin poets, later on he occasionally permitted himself a Latin expression, such as *solicitus timor, pari passu* or *casus conscientiæ.* His references to the literature cover a wide field, but they are for the most part allusions of the most casual character. The "golden age" of Roman literature is represented in his novels by Cicero, Horace, Catullus, and Vergil; and Ovid and Marcus Antoninus supply mottoes for sections of *Jude the Obscure.*

In this account of the artistic influence of the classics, some notice must be taken of Hardy's frequent repudiation of what he terms "the Greek point of view" in art, as it might otherwise seem somewhat audacious, in dealing with the ancient echoes that sound through his greatest work, to attempt to prove a proposition the validity of which the author himself may be said specifically to have denied.

The attitude which he assumed and defended is most clearly shown in two fairly well-known passages; one from *The Return of the Native,* the other from the preface to *The Dynasts.* The former attempts to contrast the general Greek attitude towards life with the modern viewpoint; the latter points out the great gulf

which, supposedly, separates the purely artistic ideals
and methods of the Greeks from those of Hardy:

> The view of life as a thing to be put up with, replacing the
> zest for existence which was so intense in early civilizations, must
> ultimately enter so thoroughly into the constitution of the ad-
> vanced races that its facial expression will become accepted as a
> new artistic departure. . . .
>
> The truth seems to be that a long line of disillusive centuries
> has permanently replaced the Hellenic ideal of life, or whatever
> it may be called. What the Greeks only suspected we know well;
> what their Æschylus imagined our nursery children feel. That
> old-fashioned revelling in the general situation grows less and
> less possible as we uncover the defects of natural laws, and see
> the quandary man is in by their operation.

Both of the assumptions upon which the above excerpt
is based are very emphatically open to question. In the
first place, was the early "zest for existence" any more
intense than it is to-day? The truth seems to be that outside of the Far-Eastern countries, which have for century after century clung to their ingrained notions of
determinism and the inevitability of destiny, the "love
of life" is as strong and universal a trait of mankind as
ever. The fatalism expressed by East-Indian soldiers
on the western front in the war struck the British with
whom they came in contact as something remarkable and
as a curiosity worth writing about—not as a view of life
that had already become universal. Even a rather superficial acquaintance with the attitude of the latest voices
in the poetry of to-day will lead one to believe that the
unreasonable and unreasoning zest for existence is growing stronger and stronger in man as the tragedy of one

generation is succeeded and exceeded by that of the next
—and this applies in almost equal measure to contemporary English novelists, with one notable exception:
Hardy himself. Modern drama, however, tells a somewhat different story, with cynicism rampant in comedy
and with tragedy saturated, as always, with a pessimism
seldom exceeded even by Schopenhauer's intellectual
plunges into the depths of human existence. But tragedy
by its essential nature presupposes catastrophe, and its
success has always been in direct proportion to the vio-
lence with which the crack of doom bursts over the heads
of the protagonists. It is perhaps true that we are to-day
somewhat more familiar with disillusive reasoning, and
that pessimistic utterances have a more familiar ring to
our ears; but that the average thinking person accepts
these ideas and conforms his life to the conclusions they
indicate, is highly questionable.

Scholars who have devoted their lives to the study of
the all too scanty remains of classical literature will
probably be very slow to admit that the average reflective Greek thinker indulged in any "revelling in the
general situation" to the degree which Hardy supposed.
Of course the Greeks were a sanguine people, particularly after the national will had been stiffened by the suc-
cesses of the Persian wars, but this great outburst of vitality has since been duplicated by other nations with
much the same degree of "high spirits." One need only
mention two familiar instances—the great Elizabethan
literature, a veritable "revelling" in optimism, which
followed the crushing of Spanish sea power by England,
and the ascendance of the German drama after the

Franco-Prussian war. Hardy seemed almost unconscious of the very deep-seated strain of disillusionment
and pessimism which runs through the greater part of
early Greek literature. A short monograph by Dr. An-
ton Baumstark, for instance, takes the very fragmentary
remains of Greek lyric poetry still extant, and turns up
an amazing display of melancholy utterances. Herbert
L. Stewart has likewise taken exception to Hardy's attitude here, and has noted that he is sometimes unfortunate in his Greek allusions. In calling attention to the
statement in one of the novels, that "ideal Greek beauty
went with Greek sanguineness of temperament," Mr.
Stewart noted that there was a deep tone of sadness in
the temperament which Hardy thought so sanguine, and
referred to Professor Butcher's essay, *The Melancholy
of the Greeks,* for confirmation of this statement.

The second pronouncement which must be disposed of
is the following:

> The scheme of contrasted choruses and other conventions of
> this eternal feature was shaped with a single view to modern ex-
> pression of a modern outlook, and in frank divergence from
> classical and other dramatic precedent which ruled the ancient
> voicings of ancient themes.

The field of investigation opened by this quotation is
a large and many-sided one, and cannot be discussed in
great detail here. It might be well to point out, however,
that one who attempts to compare the form of *The Dynasts* with that of the Greek drama need not be disturbed
or embarrassed by Hardy's repudiation of Greek influence. His choruses, though transfigured, still remain

choruses, and the function of a chorus is the same to-day
as it was yesterday. The same will be found to apply to
other ancient dramatic precedents now seldom used, but
revived and adapted by Mr. Hardy to his gigantic scheme
and then disclaimed. As to the observance of the various
species of dramatic decorum, and other classical and
pseudo-classical requirements, it may possibly be shown
that *The Dynasts,* considered as a play, is more nearly
related to the most ancient type of Athenian drama than
to the usual play of the present time. Of course no one
will attempt to deny the essential "modernity" of *The
Dynasts*—it has been hailed by philosophers of the day
as one of the few combinations of modern poetry and an
up-to-date view of life—but the terms "modern" and
"ancient" are sometimes less than valueless when used
as criteria to judging serious intellectual works of any
period. Original ideas of any time can nearly always be
regarded in two lights—as restatements of something
that had already been hinted at, and as foreshadowings
of later developments. Certain great and insoluble
problems have ever attracted speculative poets, whose
reactions have generally varied not so much according
to the age in which they lived as according to the general type of temperament and intellect they represented
—and these contrasted general types have repeated themselves since the invention of writing. The invocation of
comparisons of certain aspects of Hardy's genius and
the ideals of the oldest Greek tragedy will perhaps be regarded as a not entirely unreasonable procedure if these
considerations are borne in mind.

Turning now to the investigation of the extent of the

acquaintance with Continental European literature displayed by the author of the Wessex Novels, one will find that he is limited to the French and German of comparatively recent times, as is only to be expected—notwithstanding the fact that he may here and there make a casual allusion to Dante's *Inferno* in describing a scene, or the fact that that character-monstrosity, Dare, in *A Laodicean,* may quote Italian and Spanish proverbs to show that he is a real citizen of the world.

French expressions, phrases, and proverbs, such as *en l'air, coup d'œil, incredules les plus credules, raison d'être, ensemble, tête-à-tête,* and so on, are very common, and show at least a superficial acquaintance with the language, although they might perhaps be regarded by purists as barbaric impedimenta to a good English prose style. A more agreeable effect, perhaps, is made by his occasional introduction of a French song into the story. Thus, in *A Pair of Blue Eyes,* Elfride sings, *"Je l'ai planté, je l'ai vu naîtré,"* etc., to Stephen Smith; in *Two on a Tower,* the worldly-wise Louis Glanville sings in an undertone, *"Tra deri, dera, L'histoire n'est pas nouvelle!"* The best and most famous example, however, is Clym's singing of *"Le point du jour,"* as he works as a furze-cutter in *The Return of the Native.*

References to the literature of France are not numerous. There is passing mention of the "delicate imposition" of Rochefoucauld and of *"la jalousie rétrospectif"* of George Sand. More important is the acquaintance shown with the sceptical ratiocinations of the *Dictionnaire Philosophique* and with the symbolist and decadent schools of modern French poetry.

The Novelist (1870-1898)

If we disregard for the moment the influence of German philosophical writers upon his later work, it will be found that in the field of German the extent of his acquaintance is of about the same scope as his acquaintance with the French. Dare, of course, shows off his cosmopolitanism by saying: *Hörensagen ist halb gelogen;* Mrs. Charmond is said to have a *weltbürgerliche* nature; the Melancholy Hussar speaks of his *Heimweh;* and Alec D'Urberville gets back his old *Weltlust* after his temporary "conversion" has spent itself. The quaint lines of the lyric *Lieb' Liebchen* (in translation) are employed as an index to the agitating emotions of Lady Constantine's heart, and Börne's observation, *Nichts ist dauernd als der Wechsel,* made famous by its employment as the motto of Heine's *Harzreise,* is used to make clear the author's conception of the elusiveness of the objects of idealistic love.

If it were not for the very definite evidences of Hardy's reading in the German philosophers encountered in the novels from the year 1887 onward, one might be justified in denying to him anything but the merest smattering of German. But *The Woodlanders* contains unmistakable evidences of the influence of the Nineteenth Century transcendentalists; in *Tess of the D'Urbervilles* one can follow out with some degree of accuracy the path of Schopenhauer's inroads on Hardy's thought and its expression; and in *Jude the Obscure,* Humboldt and others come to the fore.

It would be pointing out the very obvious to show in any detail Hardy's familiarity with the great English writers, from Sir Thomas Wyatt to Swinburne. Not only the more "literary" types of poetic composition claim his attention, but also such things as the old ballads, folk-plays and the saints' legends. The great Elizabethan outburst of literature fascinated him, and Shakespeare is mentioned in nearly every novel. With Milton he was, of course, familiar, and, among a host of other well-known figures that appear in his pages, he singled Defoe out for his especial admiration. Of the leaders of the great Romantic movement of the early Nineteenth Century he was particularly fond of Shelley, Coleridge, and Keats; and Wordsworth stimulated his interest, if not always his approval. Tennyson and Browning came in chiefly for criticism of their "optimism," Rosetti for his typically Pre-Raphaelitish absurdities of expression. Of American writers he mentioned Poe and Whitman. Although Hardy, as a writer, was singularly independent of "literary influences," echoes of Shakespeare, Milton (especially in *The Dynasts*), and Shelley can sometimes be heard in his poems, and his enthusiasm for the matter-of-fact but vivid and individual prose style, and the fearless realism of Defoe was undoubtedly responsible in large measure for those qualities as they are found in his fiction.

The modern literary world is presented from the amateur writer's standpoint in most interesting fashion in the discussion of Elfride's Gothic Romance: *The Court of Kellyon Castle,* and of Ethelberta's publication of her efforts in the writing of *vers de societé,* a book "teeming with ideas bright as mirrors and just as unsubstantial . . . to justify the ways of girls to men."

Hardy had very little to say directly of his opinions on

the art of poetry itself, but the little that he did say is of the utmost significance. In the first place, he took pains to combat the popular notion of the poet and the poet's life. For instance, when Christopher Julian's simple-minded sister, Faith, is asked if Ethelberta is really a poetess, she replies, "That I cannot say. She is very clever at verses; but she don't lean over gates to see the sun, and goes to church as regular as you or I, so I should hardly be inclined to say that she's the complete thing. . . ." One may notice also the following bit of burlesque dialogue in *The Hand of Ethelberta,* in which the same fallacious views of the practice of poetry are ridiculed with rather broad satirical strokes:

After a pause Neigh remarked half-privately to their host, who was his uncle: "Your butler Chickerel is a very intelligent man, as I have heard."

"Yes, he does very well," said Mr. Doncastle.

"But is he not a—very extraordinary man?"

"Not to my knowledge," said Doncastle, looking up surprised. "Why do you think that, Alfred?"

"Well, perhaps it was not a matter to mention. He reads a great deal, I dare say?"

"I don't think so."

"I noticed how wonderfully his face kindled when we began talking about the poems during dinner. Perhaps he is a poet himself in disguise. Did you observe it?"

"No. To the best of my belief he is a very trustworthy and honorable man. He has been with us—let me see, how long?— five months, I think, and he was fifteen years in his last place. It certainly is a new side to his character if he publicly showed any interest in the conversation, whatever he may have felt."

"Since the matter has been mentioned," said Mr. Jones, "I may say that I too noticed the singularity of it."

The Life of Thomas Hardy

"If you had not said otherwise," replied Doncastle somewhat warmly, "I should have asserted him to be the last man-servant in London to infringe such an elementary rule. If he did so this evening, it is certainly for the first time, and I sincerely hoped that no annoyance was caused—"

"O no, no—not at all—it might have been a mistake of mine," said Jones. "I should quite have forgotten the circumstances if Mr. Neigh's words had not brought it to my mind. It was really nothing to notice, and I beg that you will not say a word to him on my account."

Application of the qualities discovered in a poet's writing to the character of the poet himself is a process of reasoning that Hardy often characterized as fallacious. Sue tells Jude that "some of the most passionately erotic poets have been the most self-contained in their daily lives." There are evidences, on the other hand, that he did not think very highly of emotional poetry produced by phlegmatic temperaments. Thus Ethelberta begins as a poet of a rather sweetened Satanic school, but as experiences accumulate, she begins to wonder if her early notes "had the genuine ring in them, or whether a poet who could be thrust by realities to a distance beyond recognition as such was a true poet at all." The author goes on to hint that the distorted Benthamism with which she justifies her subsequent course may be, ethically considered, superior to her original playful Romanticism. One may here call to mind the complete absence of the typical Romantic emotionalism from Hardy's own lyrics, from even his avowed "love-lyrics." No one can possibly consider him a "passionately erotic" poet, and very few would go so far as defi-

The Novelist (1870-1898)

nitely to call his verse "emotional," if by that term is meant the unpremeditated overflow of feeling, untinctured by reason. Romantic love is conspicuously absent from the scheme of *The Dynasts,* and when it is treated in the lyrics, there is nearly always running through it that kind of matured and disillusioned insight that finds its classic expression in Schopenhauer's *Metaphysics of the Love of the Sexes.* Of course, this does not mean that emotion is absent—the poet shows unmistakably that he feels, but he cannot help showing at the same time that he knows the "whence" and the "wherefore" of his feeling. This may help one to understand Springrove's statement that the writing of emotional verses was a stage that some types of young men must pass through, as they pass through the stage of shaving for a beard.

Besides his opposition to sentimentalism in modern poetry, Hardy sometimes expressed a total lack of appreciation of the production of beautiful sounds in poetry for their own sake. The sense, the idea of a composition was to him the main consideration, and was not to be subordinated to the texture of the material with which it was presented. The form should always suit the matter; therefore a poet must be a master of the technique of his craft; but his technical dexterity should never be permitted to detract the reader's attention from the things he really wants to say; if he has nothing to say, he should not manufacture beautiful sounds in order to say it. Thus we find him writing, four years after the first *Poems and Ballads* of Swinburne had started a cult of sound for sound's sake, "The conversation was naturally at first of a nervous, tentative kind, in which, as in the works of some minor poets, the sense was considerably led by the sound." The same opinion was expressed somewhat later in *An Imaginative Woman,* in which the poetic activities described as belonging to Robert Trewe might be considered as rather faithful reflections of the author's:

> Being little attracted by excellences of form and rhythm apart from content he sometimes, when feeling outran his artistic speed, perpetrated sonnets in the loosely rhymed Elizabethan fashion, which every right-minded reviewer said he ought not to have done.

Hardy's description of other aspects of the poetry of the fictitious Robert Trewe opens the general question of the relationship between poetry and life, and brings one again to the scarred battlefields where the opposing armies of realism and romanticism have fought many a fight:

> Trewe's verse contrasted with that of the rank and file of recent minor poets in being impassioned rather than ingenious, luxuriant rather than finished. Neither symboliste nor decadent, he was a pessimist in so far as that character applies to a man who looks at the worst contingencies as well as the best in the human condition.

Hardy's own opinion in the matter is perhaps more directly and forcibly expressed in *Tess,* when, in dealing with the miserable and undeserved lot of the children of the shiftless Durbeyfields in being born into the world in such circumstances as theirs, he remarks, with a quite perceptible sneer, "some people would like to know

The Novelist (1870-1898)

whence the poet whose philosophy is in these days deemed as profound and trustworthy as his verse is tonic and breezy gets his authority for speaking of 'Nature's holy plan.' "

As a sincere disciple of realism Hardy aimed always to give "a fairly true picture, at first hand, of the personages, ways, and customs" of the characters he created. This picture of humanity as it really is he framed in a nature-setting that was the result of the closest and sharpest observation, refined and interpreted by the deepest possible insight. But he was not merely a realistic photographer of scenes and impressions. His essentially romantic insight often enabled him to pierce through the surface of the material things and invest them with a personality that is often more striking and more vividly presented than the human agents. Egdon Heath is of course the supreme example of this, but to the discerning reader the rural fragrance of *Under the Greenwood Tree,* the cliff and the storm in *A Pair of Blue Eyes,* the lonely observatory surrounded by the ever-sighing pines in *Two on a Tower,* and the ancient Roman amphitheatre in *The Mayor of Casterbridge,* are *dramatis personæ* whose distinctive qualities linger in the mind long after many of the human characters have faded out of memory. If the essential Romantic is, in the words of Lawrence Gilman, "he, who, piercing the illusory veil of material fact, reveals to us, through symbol and imagery, the enduring soul of wonder and enchantment which inhabits the world," then Hardy is, at least in his treatment of the external world, an essential Romantic.

His greatness as a novelist is probably due, however,

to his recognized insight into the workings of the human heart. That he possessed no mean power of psychological analysis of motives is shown by many a passage in his very first novels. Sometimes his expression of a quite common and simple observation could be altogether delightful in its simplicity, as when

Dick wondered how it was that when people were married they could be so blind to romance; and was quite certain that if he ever took to wife that dear impossible Fancy, he and she would never be so dreadfully practical and undemonstrative of their passion as his father and mother were. The most extraordinary thing was, that all the fathers and mothers he knew were just as undemonstrative as his own.

More subtle analysis is seen in the following:

There exists as it were an outer chamber of the mind, in which, when a man is occupied centrally with the most momentous question of his life, casual and trifling thoughts are just allowed to wander softly for an interval, before being banished altogether.

Despite his constant and consistent aim at truth to life, he departed, at the outset of his career, from the rock-bound principles of the stricter Naturalists, in his advocation of the principles of the necessary selection and artistic ordering of the facts of life as observed, in order to reproduce, as the resultant effect, the writer's personal interpretation of the ultimate significance, or non-significance, of things in general. Thus we find him in full accord with the most famous novelist of the English Romanticists in the motto he prefixed to *Desperate Remedies:*

A page from the manuscript of *A Group of Noble Dames*. The original manuscript of *A Group of Noble Dames* was presented to the Library of Congress, Washington, D. C., by Mr. Hardy at the suggestion of Mr. Sydney Carlyle Cockerell, M.A., Curator of the Fitzwilliam Museum, Cambridge, England. In a letter to Mr. Cockerell, dated October 11, 1911, Hardy referred to the gift in the following terms:

"I am rather appalled at the temerity of presenting these old MSS and should much like it to appear on each record or label in some way either that they were presented through you, at your wish or suggestion, or presented to you to distribute as you should choose. It would, I feel, not be quite becoming for a writer to send his MSS to a Museum on his own judgment."

The Novelist (1870-1898)

"Though a course of adventures which are only connected with each other by having happened to the same individual is what most frequently occurs in nature, yet the province of the romance-writer being artificial, there is more required from him than a mere compliance with the simplicity of reality."—SIR WALTER SCOTT.

It would naturally be the greatest possible fallacy to assume that Hardy's sympathy with the ideals of the historical romancers went very far. There is indeed a vast gulf between *Quentin Durward* and *The Trumpet-Major*. The idea of "poetic justice" and the inevitable happy ending was claimed by Hardy to be absolutely inconsistent with honesty to the facts or to the significance of life. One of his earliest bits of literary criticism was a palpable sneer at "the indiscriminate righting of everything at the end of an old play," although in the novel in which it occurs, everything turns out fairly well in the end. Realism, even though it involves the acceptance of a rather distasteful pessimism, is defended by the tranter, Reuben Dewy, who, in the discussion of Michael Mail's sometimes rather unsavory stories, remarks:

". . . That sort o' coarse touch that's so upsetting to Ann's feelings is to my mind a recommendation; for it do always prove a story to be true. And for the same rayson, I like a story with a bad moral. My sonnies, all true stories have a coarseness or a bad moral, depend upon't. If the story-tellers could ha' got decency and good morals from true stories, who'd ha' troubled to invent parables?" . . .

In the search after truth, Hardy maintained that no previous general conceptions of "what ought to be" should be permitted to influence the full recognition of the facts themselves as such. Not until a view of life has actually been distilled from close observation, and fixed through insight and ratiocination, should it be employed in influencing the artistic selection, ordering, and presentation of impressions. Henry Knight comes to grief chiefly because of his failure to observe this principle:

> The moral rightness of this man's life was worthy of all praise; but in spite of some intellectual acumen, Knight had in him a modicum of that wrongheadedness which is mostly found in scrupulously honest people. With him, truth seemed too clean and pure an abstraction to be so hopelessly churned in with error as practical persons find it.

Hardy hinted that Shakespeare himself did not follow out the principle of "poetic justice" in *Romeo and Juliet* and *Othello*. *King Lear* and *The Return of the Native* are both great poetry and they are both true to life, but they both present a view of life that is not particularly appealing to the optimistic idealist and romantic.

The novelist's criticism of the subject matter and technique of fiction is found in its most concentrated form in the articles which he contributed to various periodicals between 1888 and 1891. In them he defended his sincere search for truth, accompanied by an attentive ear for the "still sad music of humanity" that ultimately makes all writing such as his own worth while. In this latter respect his aims differed from those of Zola and other purely scientific realists.

The Novelist (1870-1898)

A steady growth of self-consciousness as a literary artist seems to have taken place in Hardy, from the time of his first "disillusioned" verses onwards. Like his own "Immanent Will," he seems very gradually to have gained cognition and consciousness of the movements of which he was a part. By the late nineties he probably realized, not that he was part of a movement of scepticism and pessimism, but that the freedom from illusion of the time was, curiously, in agreement with the sardonic point of view that he had already developed and expressed.

CHAPTER VIII

THE LYRIC POET (1898-1922)

*W*HEN Hardy's first volume of poems, *Wessex Poems,* appeared in 1898, illustrated with sketches by the author, now approaching his sixtieth year, everyone was disposed to regard it as an interesting but not particularly valuable illustration of a great novelist's self-entertainment by means of incidental experiments with art and poetry. When, three years later, his next book proved to be *Poems of the Past and the Present,* readers began to suspect that his career as a novelist might have to be considered as definitely closed. The most current speculation as to the probable cause of this rather unexpected turn of affairs was that Hardy had been disgusted and disheartened by the adverse and hysterical criticism leveled against *Jude.* As it was humorously put in Max Beerbohm's burlesque *Sequelula to The Dynasts*:

Spirit of the Years

. . . And lately, I believe,
Another parasite has had the impudence
To publish an elaborate account
Of our (for so we deemed it) private visit.

Spirit Sinister

His name?

[190]

The Lyric Poet (1898-1922)

Recording Angel

One moment.
>   (Turns over the leaves.)
>   *Hardy.   Mr. Thomas.*
Novelist. Author of The Woodlanders,
Far from the Madding Crowd, The Trumpet-Major,
Tess of the D'Urbervilles, etcetera,
Etcetera. In 1895
Jude the Obscure was published, and a few
Hasty reviewers, having to supply
A column for the day of publication
Filled out their space by saying that there were
Several passages that might have been
Omitted with advantage. Mr. Hardy
Saw that if that was so, well then, of course,
Obviously the only thing to do
Was to write no more novels, and forthwith
Applied himself to Drama, and to Us. . . .

Mr. Beerbohm really thought, however, that "to accept that explanation were to insult him. A puny engine of art may be derailed by such puny obstacles as the public can set in its way. So strong an engine as Mr. Hardy rushes straight on, despite them, never so little jarred by them, and stops not save for lack of inward steam. Mr. Hardy writes no more novels because he has no more novels to write."

The most reasonable explanation seems to be that Hardy, feeling that he had expressed himself in the form of prose fiction as well as he was ever likely to, and that he had sufficiently indulged the public in using for twenty-five years the most easily comprehended method of approach, decided that he would henceforth indulge himself by employing the form of literary art in which it had ever been his ambition to become a master. His novels had assured him of income and position; he could now afford to speculate in the hazardous field of poetry.

Some people, indeed, had already realized that they had been reading poetry while they perused the "novels of character and environment," and accepted the new state of affairs with satisfaction. Others, however, simply stopped reading Hardy. At any rate, the world had before long to assimilate the fact that if it wanted to read Hardy's new books, it would have to read verse.

Poems of the Past and the Present, like *Wessex Poems,* contained many early pieces, but consisted chiefly of Hardy's poetical efforts between 1898 and 1901, recording his impressions of the Boer War and of two trips to Italy, the *Poems of Pilgrimage. Time's Laughingstocks* appeared in 1909; it was distinguished by *A Set of Country Songs,* some of the most successful dramatic ballads, the *Love Lyrics* and the greater part of those poems in which the ancient Wessex musicians reappear in person and in spirit. *Satires of Circumstance* followed in 1914; it has, without too much exaggeration, been called one of the most remarkable collections of poetry produced in recent years. It drew forth the following comment from Mr. Gosse:

This seems to be the *Troilus and Cressida* of his life's work, the book in which he is revealed most distracted by conjecture and most overwhelmed by the miscarriage of everything. The wells of human hope have been poisoned for him by some condition of which we know nothing, and even the picturesque features of Dorsetshire landscape that have always before dispersed

The Lyric Poet (1898-1922)

his melancholy, fail to win his attention. The strongest of the poems of disillusion which are the outcome of his mood, is *The Newcomer's Wife,* with the terrible abruptness of its final stanza. . . . At all events, one must welcome a postscript in which a blast on the bugle of war seemed to have wakened the poet from his dark brooding to the sense of a new chapter in history.

Whether or not this conjecture hits the truth of the matter, no one was prepared to deny that *Satires of Circumstance,* and in particular the "fifteen glimpses" that give the volume its title, produced upon the reader an effect of tragic pity and horror unequaled by anything else in the works of this modern master of tragedy, unless it be some of the more gruesome scenes in *The Dynasts,* or in *Jude the Obscure.* A tangible clue to the personal significance of the volume to its author was afforded by the memorable group of *Poems of 1912-13,* in which the death of Mrs. Hardy and the poet's bereavement were recorded with a beauty, pathos, and peculiar emotional restraint that frequently equals, and occasionally surpasses, the finest pieces done in a similar vein by Wordsworth. The volume also contained the famous lines on the loss of the *Titanic, The Convergence of the Twain,* and, as first published, closed with Hardy's first lyric of the Great War, *Men Who March Away.*

If *Satires of Circumstance* was the most sharply tragic of Hardy's books of lyrics, *Moments of Vision* rose to far greater heights in ripeness of thought, beauty of imagery, and perfection of form. Here Hardy at last achieved, with consummate artistry, that perfect adaptation of language and structure to the intellectual, dramatic, or lyric content of the poems, toward which he had

striven since his earliest attempts at versification. It
was a book that but few could enjoy at a first reading,
but the strange rhythmic cadences, the seemingly per-
verse and distorted handling of the language, and the
delicate and unusual variations on the Hardy-situations
and the Hardy-philosophy that one learned to look for,
finally exercised a charm that completely dispelled all
memory of the impression of queerness that distracted
the reader at first. Except for the collection of war-
poems at the end, the book, as well as the *Late Lyrics
and Earlier* (1922), consisted entirely of miscellaneous
and entirely undated pieces.

*   *

*

Although the characteristics noted above serve to distinguish the volumes from each other, these books present, in general, such uniform qualities in technique, material, and content, that a chronological arrangement of
the later lyrics seems rather futile. To follow out such
an arrangement would, at all events, be almost an impossibility, as Hardy took care to date but very few of his
poems. It is all one can do to extricate the very early
poems from the mass of the later, "post-fictional" material. Hardy's aims, both artistic and intellectual, have
been singularly steady and consistent through his long
career, and while his later work seems to show an increasing facility and sureness of touch, his objectives remain substantially the same as they were when he ceased
merely experimenting and began to write poetry in earnest. One finds the same kind of criticism leveled at

The Lyric Poet (1898-1922)

Moments of Vision that was first directed against *Wessex Poems* and then against *The Dynasts,* and one can find, to a lesser degree, in *Wessex Poems* many of the qualities that raise *Satires of Circumstance* and *Moments of Vision* to the rank of "great poetry."

Before attacking the subject-matter which the poet uses, or the aspect and inner significance of the poetic edifice he has raised, the questions connected with his purely technical qualifications for executing the tasks of a lyrist must be disposed of. The language, style, and verse-structure of Hardy's lyric poems have caused more than one critic and sincere reader to throw down his books and refuse to attempt to penetrate further into the mysteries of poetry that presented such an uncouth and forbidding exterior.

Hardy's choice and use of English words in his poems has provoked and irritated many a commentator, and is a subject that demands rather close and extended comment, in spite of the warning example of George Meredith's dull professor, who "pores over a little inexactitude in phrases and pecks at it like a domestic fowl." The guiding principle that is undoubtedly at the base of Hardy's handling of the language is that of using at all times the exact and precise word for the expression of an idea. The sense of a passage, whether of prose or verse, and the clearness of the picture or impression to be conveyed, are never to be sacrificed to the sound—to the purely sensory appeal of the language. This has been noticed even by readers of his prose, and has already been discovered to be one of his few definitely expressed tenets on the subject of poetic composition. It may be of some interest to compare this theory of Hardy's, and its application in his poems, with the first article in the creed of our present-day Imagist school, which reads: "To use the language of common speech, but to employ always the exact word, not the nearly-exact, nor the merely decorative word." With the latter—and more important—part of this fundamental tenet, Hardy is entirely in sympathy, but is his language that of common speech? In the novels, certainly. Nowhere in his prose, which is usually of a sublime simplicity, can one find such a monstrosity as this notorious and frequently quoted passage perpetrated by Meredith,—the speech of an eighteen-year-old girl: "We have met. It is more than I have merited. We part. In mercy let it be forever. Oh, terrible word! Coined by the passions of our youth, it comes to us for our sole riches when we are bankrupt of earthly treasures, and is the passport given by Abnegation unto Woe that prays to quit this probationary sphere."

But what of Hardy's verse? Let us open the *Wessex Poems,* or the *Collected Poems,* and glance at the very first stanza of the very first poem:

> Change and chancefulness in my flowering youthtime,
> Set me sun by sun near to one unchosen;
> Wrought us fellowlike, and despite divergence
>   Fused us in friendship.

Certainly this is not the language of common, nor of uncommon, speech. There are those who will perhaps deny that it is language at all. The trouble does not lie in the fact that it is a rather unsuccessful attempt to

The Lyric Poet (1898-1922)

make correct Sapphic stanzas sound smooth in English (which Swinburne proved could be done), but the perplexity of the reader begins before he has had time to recognize the metrical scheme. The word *chancefulness* stops him almost as soon as he begins to read. He then stumbles a bit over *unchosen,* but reads on, until stopped again by *fellowlike.* Upon repeated readings he will, if he is persistent, gradually divine the poet's meaning, grow accustomed to the curious cadences of the verse, and finally will experience a distinct pleasure in reperusing the piece. The cardinal stumbling-block to an appreciation of Hardy's lyric poetry is undoubtedly the effort exacted of the reader by the seemingly uncouth words habitually employed. Trained linguists have observed, however, that Hardy is very rarely indeed responsible for the actual coinage or invention of a new word, and that in the few cases in which he produces a new form, it is invariably evolved logically out of established and known elements of the language. His practice is not, for the most part, that of word-manufacture, but of word-preservation. Unconsciously following the example of the celebrated Hariri and other Arabic poets and men of letters who devoted their lives to the preservation of their ancient language in all its marvellous flexibility, he attempts to enliven the English of modern poetry through the systematic but always felicitous introduction of antique and pseudo-antique forms and expressions. In the fulfilment of this aim he consistently reverts to the native, or Anglo-Saxon, element of the language, and very rarely resurrects an old French derivative. The *hapax legomena* of Hardy are almost invariably old English words, or, less frequently, direct descendants of Greek or Latin originals.

This Teutonic, as distinguished from the Celtic or Romance viewpoint with regard to the history and future development of English is not without some significance for the study of Hardy's larger *"Weltanschauung."* Again we discover his spirit to be *en rapport* with the ancient inhabitants of Wessex, the genius of whose country has always exercised such a firm hold upon him.

Among critics it was fashionable, until a very short time ago, to point the finger of scorn at Hardy's efforts in versification. His technique as a prose-novelist has always evoked admiration for its purity and sureness of touch, but these qualities do not seem to have been so easily discoverable in his poetry. Even so acute an appraiser of contemporary literature as Richard Le Gallienne, while admitting Hardy's claim to greatness, dismissed his verse by calling it "poetry-in-travail rather than poetry delivered." Lawrence Binyon probed the matter somewhat more deeply, when he observed that the mechanism of a Hardy-stanza "creaks and groans with the pressure of its working," and that "there is something incongruous between the prosaic plainness of speech and the tight structure of the rather elaborate lyric form to which it is trimmed." The recognition of Hardy's merits and demerits as a versifier will, perhaps fortunately, depend ultimately on the examples of his art that he has himself produced, rather than on the hastily formed opinions of his first readers.

No one will ever claim for Hardy's poetry the golden melody of a Shelley or a Burns, nor the symphonic splen-

The Lyric Poet (1898-1922)

dor of sound that belongs to the works of Keats and Swinburne; he makes no direct appeal to the ear of his reader. But after repeated readings of his lyrics the first fantastic grotesqueness of effect wears off, leaving at times a fascinatingly pungent quality that is seen finally to be the inevitable medium for the thought that is expressed. His more prosy lyrics should not be viewed as wilful distortions of set and elaborate measures, but should be read as naturally as is consistent with the preservation of their symmetry. Then, as the syncopations, misplaced quantities and compensations outnumber the consonances, the effect will approach that of free verse and prose-poetry. In its rhythmic freedom, and in its forsaking of sweetness of melody for its own sake, Hardy's mature poetry is perhaps analogous to the work of many modern musicians, who are indulging in unheard-of dissonances, and whose rhythmic complexities have broken away from all metronomic restraints.

There seems to be little doubt that the natural and free forms of Oriental poetry have recently made a tremendous impress upon contemporary poets, whose work has heretofore been of strictly geometric patterns, both simple and complex. The unforced cadences of speech are perhaps winning the fight over the old-fashioned artificiality too easily for the health of the art—but there is no danger if the contest is really between the mechanical, straight-edged architecture of man and the unconscious artistry of nature. However that may be, Hardy's sense of form, developed by his earliest profession and applied throughout a long career of prose-writing, did not forsake him when he turned to composition in verse. He scheme of things was also comprehended. There was no experience and no event too trivial, and none too imposing, to find a record in Hardy's lyrics. The whole range of his interests and of his ideas achieved expression here, as well as his immediate imaginative reaction to events of the time, nowhere recorded in his prose works.

Some of these poems showed Hardy in an entirely new light—that of a "laureate" poet; but the most obviously "occasional" pieces demonstrated once for all the fact that that official distinction could never be his. The passing of Edward VII and the accession of the present George called forth two notable poems. For *A King's Soliloquy—On the Night of His Funeral* was a lament over the unfruitfulness, "the days of drudgery, the nights of stress" of the life of a monarch, even when he is determined to get the best of all the enjoyments that his extraordinary opportunities put within his reach;— the "average track of average men" is to be preferred —and the poem ends on a fatalistic note:

> Something binds hard the royal hand,
>   As all that be,
> And it is That has shaped, has planned
>   My acts and me.

The Coronation was a most extraordinary working-out of an idea that might have been molded into a masterpiece. The older rulers of the island are awakened by the noises of the erection of the temporary scaffolding for the ceremony at Westminster, and speculate on the significance of the disturbance. The reader speculates just as vainly on the meaning, or "point" of the poem itself, and the crudity, both of expression and of technique, is apt to cause some embarrassment to the Hardy-enthusiast. Here is a choice selection of the royal dialogue:

"—Perhaps a scaffold!" Mary Stuart sighed,
"If such still be. It was that way I died."

—"Ods! Far more like," said the many-wived,
"That for a wedding 'tis this work's contrived."

"Ha-ha! I never would bow down to Rimmon,
But a had a rare time with those six women!"

"Not all at once?" gasped he who loved confession.
"Nay, nay!" said Hal. "That would have been transgression."

"—They build a catafalque here, black and tall,
Perhaps," mused Richard, "for some funeral?"

And Anne chimed in: "Ah, yes: it may be so!"
"Nay!" squeaked Eliza. "Little you seem to know—

"Clearly 'tis for some crowning here in state,
As they crowned us at our long by gone date. . . ." etc.

One does not wonder that patriotic British journals did not scramble for Hardy's poetical comment on news of the day;—what would the average Londoner have thought of his morning paper, if, on the day after the coronation, "Eliza" had "squeaked" at him from the printed lines that represented the laureate's celebration of the event? . . . To say nothing of the gracelessness

The Lyric Poet (1898-1922)

of bringing in "Hal" and his notoriously complex domestic problems. The whole poem was a most unusual thing to find in Hardy: an example of really bad work.

A sudden and complete transition from the ridiculous to the sublime may be effected by turning to examine another occasional poem, the lines of the loss of the "Titanic," *The Convergence of the Twain.* From the first stanza,

> In a solitude of the sea
> Deep from human vanity
> And the Pride of Life that planned her, stilly couches she.

to the last,

> Till the Spinner of the Years
> Said "Now!" And each one hears,
> And consummation comes, and jars two hemispheres.

the language and the thought achieve an exaltation and a grandeur that touch the heart of the reader more forcibly and tellingly than any more sensational or sentimental treatment of the theme could possibly do. Here the "Immanent Will, that stirs and urges everything" definitely displaced the poet's earlier and more awkward conception of Chance and Time as agents of Destiny.

The ballads of the Napoleonic wars found in the *Wessex Poems* represent Hardy's continued interest in a theme that had already occasioned *The Trumpet-Major* and was eventually to find its consummation in *The Dynasts.* Edmund Gosse wrote that they were conceived, and a few lines written, long before their completion.

The Life of Thomas Hardy

Certainly they represent their author's most spontaneous work, and have drawn admiration when his other poems only succeeded in drawing sneers or other more vigorous tokens of hostility. One of the first reviewers of *Wessex Poems* went so far as to express a belief that Hardy could possibly do a great historical romance on the Napoleonic wars.

Leipzig, the tale of the taking of the city by the Allies in 1813, told by "old Norbert with the flat blue cap" on an evening in the master-tradesman's parlor at the Old Ship Inn at Casterbridge, is remarkable for its dramatic handling of the event that was to form the bulk of Act III of the third part of *The Dynasts;* for its swiftness of movement and vividness of expression that anticipated much of the vigor of execution so notably characteristic of the later poems, and for its iterated emphasis on the poet's disillusioned view of warfare:

Fifty thousand sturdy souls on those trampled plains and knolls
    Who met the dawn hopefully,
And were lotted their shares in a quarrel not theirs,
    Dropt then in their agony.

San Sebastian, again a dramatic monologue, stresses the sordid and horrid aspects of war—it is a tale of the undying remorse that clings to the spirit of a man who has committed outrages such as always accompany the taking and plundering of towns when the soldiery are released from control. *The Peasant's Confession,* likewise a tale of remorse, takes us to the field of Waterloo, and explains the failure of Grouchy to arrive on the field in time by the fact that Napoleon's messenger was betrayed and slain by a treacherous peasant. Five full stanzas are devoted to a Homeric or Æschylean catalogue of the noted fallen—a mere enumeration of the names of familiar and unfamiliar heroes. It will be seen that this is an anticipation of the technique of *The Dynasts*. The dramatic quality of the story is vividly reflected in the speed and the broken rhythms of the verses. *The Alarm* was based, like many an episode in *The Trumpet-Major*, on an actual Hardy-family tradition dealing with Bonaparte's threatened invasion of England, when all the country was in a fever of excitement and preparation.

In contrast to these poems, based on history and local legend, were those occasioned by Hardy's own experiences and observations in times of war. The "War-Poems" in *Poems of the Past and the Present* were written at various times during the Boer War, and give a picture of that struggle as viewed from Southampton, London, and Wessex. The first thing that one realizes after a mere glance through this group is that, for all his philosophic generalization, Hardy was by no means insensible to the external picturesqueness of the military spectacles he witnessed. The colorful excitement of embarcation-scenes, the tramp of a battery through rain and mud, with wives and sweethearts trudging alongside as best they may, the crowds about the war-office watching the bulletins,—all these impressions are recorded. Nor was he less alive to the inevitable and natural emotions aroused in the crowds through the stirring up of the spirit of patriotism and of the love of adventure that is a part of everyone's nature. Soldierly enthusiasm

coupled with soldierly fatalism and soldierly melancholy, breathes through the lines of *The Colonel's Soliloquy*. The many splendid dramatic possibilities were not
overlooked by any means; witness *The Going of the Battery* and *Song of the Soldiers' Wives and Sweethearts*,
which make their readers live through the anguish of
parting and the joy of meeting. The irony of events is
here represented by the characteristic *A Wife in London*,
in which the poor unfortunate receives on one day a
cablegram announcing the death of her husband, and on
the next a letter from him, full of rosy hopes and plans
for the future.

To the realization of the essentially tragic quality of
events as they affect individuals he added the disillusive
conclusions about war that force themselves upon the un-
impassioned thinker when the superficial excitement induced by the "herd instinct" has worn off. On Christmas-eve, in 1899, the poet wondered at the inconsistency
of tacking "Anno Domini" to the years that were as yet
unilluminated by that spirit of peace for which Christ
died; and the souls of the slain, in another poem written
at the same time, rushing homeward like the Pentecost-
Wind, discover to their dismay that they are remembered
for their homely and commonplace characteristics rather
than for their words and deeds of military prowess.
Hardy already longed for the time when saner, softer
policies would prevail, and patriotism scorn to stand
"bond-slave to realms, but circle earth and seas," in
the universal brotherhood of man. How far was this
spirit of lovingkindness removed from the imperialistic
bluster of Kipling!—who, with all his genius, never once

East High Street, Dorchester, showing St. Peter's Church, the bronze statue of William Barnes, the Corn Exchange and the King's Arms Hotel. From an aquatint by John Everett.

achieved the wonderful suggestion, accomplished by the employment of simple, dignified, and rhythmical language, of such a poem as *Drummer Hodge:*

> They throw in Drummer Hodge, to rest
>   Uncoffined—just as found:
> His landmark is a kopje-crest
>   That breaks the veldt around:
> And foreign constellations rest
>   Each night above his mound.
>
> Young Hodge the Drummer never knew—
>   Fresh from his Wessex home—
> The meaning of the broad Karoo,
>   The Bush, the dusty loam,
> And why uprose, to nightly view
>   Strange stars amid the gloam.
>
> Yet portion of that unknown plain
>   Will Hodge forever be,
> His homely Northern breast and brain
>   Grow to some Southern tree,
> And strange-eyed constellations reign
>   His stars eternally.

The *Sick God* closed these Boer-War poems. Here the delicious feeling of relief upon the conclusion of peace and the cessation of familiar horrors, led Hardy to the supposition that the growth of sanity and loving fellowship in humanity, (or, to translate it into the language of the Hardy-philosophy—the growth of consciousness in the all-pervading Immanent Will) was gradually bringing about a lack of interest in the art of war and an increasing feeling of disgust at its methods. Men, he felt,

were beginning to estimate the ancient pomp and circumstance of the military spirit at its true value:

Yet wars arise, though zest grows cold;
Wherefore at times, as if in ancient mould
He looms, bepatched with paint and lath;
But never hath he seemed the old!

Let men rejoice, let men deplore,
The lurid Deity of heretofore
Succumbs to one of saner nod;
The Battle-god is god no more.

Unfortunately, this note of melioristic optimism was
proved to be based on fallacious foundations by the
events that followed. It was, perhaps, the general feeling after a second-rate war, but it is a feeling that seems
to wear off with extreme rapidity under the stress of the
clash of dynasties. Hardy here unconsciously—and
therefore, perhaps, most effectively—illustrated the
irony of circumstance. The author of *Men Who March
Away* must have realized what a scurvy trick Time had
played upon him in making a "laughingstock" of *The
Sick God*.

In the year before the outbreak of the Great War
Hardy wrote the poem called *His Country,* expressing his
transcendental view of the idea of patriotism. The
synopses of all the stanzas running through marginal
notes read as follows: "He travels southward and looks
around; and cannot discover the boundary of his native
country; or where his duties to his fellow-creatures end;
nor where are his enemies." The last stanza reads:

The Lyric Poet (1898-1922)

I asked me: "Whom have I to fight,
  And whom have I to dare,
And whom to weaken, crush, and blight?
My country seems to have kept in sight
  On my way everywhere."

Thus runs the poem in its final state, as found in the
Collected Poems. On its first appearance in *Satires of
Circumstance,* however, it bore the note "Written before
the War," possibly to defend the rather patent cynicism
of the original final stanza, omitted in the definitive edition, in which "he is set right by a wise man who pities
his blindness," and which reads:

"Ah, you deceive with such pleas!"
  Said one with pitying eye.
"Foreigners—not like us—are these;
Stretch country-love beyond the seas?—
  Too Christian."—"Strange," said I.

It is futile to speculate on the reasons why a writer
who had the courage to publish *Jude,* and, during the
war, *The Pity of It,* should have seen fit to "censor" this
original conclusion to the poem. So let us proceed to the
blasts of the Hardyan bugle that accompanied the early
stages of the greatest Historical Calamity, or Conflict of
Peoples—to quote from the Preface of *The Dynasts*—
"artificially brought about in our own times."

As might have been expected of a man of seventy-four,
Hardy in this later group was no longer attracted by the
merely picturesque aspects of war. His utter repug-
nance to the methods of modern warfare was strongly
brought out in *Then and Now* (1915), which set in con-

The Life of Thomas Hardy

trast the gentlemen-warriors of earlier days, with their elevated conceptions of honor, and the contemporary Herods, who breathe:

> . . . "Sly slaughter
> Shall rule! Let us, by modes once called accurst,
> Overhead, under water,
> Stab first."

The one enduring feature of all his war-poetry was his continual praise of the simple heart and the simple faith of the common soldier who neither instigates hatred nor philosophizes about it, but who does the fighting, feels the pain of it all, and uncomplainingly makes the best of it. The "Song of the Soldiers," *Men Who March Away,* written September 5, 1914, gave poignant expression to the natural and unforced patriotic faith and fire that burn in the hearts of those who are ready to die for their belief that "Victory crowns the just." Instinctive insular patriotism continued to exercise its sway over Hardy even so late as 1917, when we find him writing *A Call to National Service,* a sonnet that urged his countrymen on to unceasing efforts even though the struggle was bringing forth signs of exhaustion;—it shows the really tremendous strength of his patriotic instincts, that overwhelmed completely his finely wrought transcendental schemes for the "brotherhood of man." *England to Germany in 1914* likewise concluded with the sort of sentiment that one expects from the orator who appeals to the national spirit of his audience. Yet one can hardly say that Hardy ever clearly or forcibly sounded the note of hatred of enemies.

The Lyric Poet (1898-1922)

The whole group of war-poems ends on a rather forbidding note: the poet's vigorous renunciation of the instinctive joy in life that makes him "want to write a book" in a world so full of horrors that the truly wise man should want to drown himself as did the father of a son slain in battle.

A remarkable complexity of emotion and ratiocination was here exhibited. Loyalty to his native country and indignation against her enemies alternated with feelings of horror at the suffering and misery caused by the irrational patriotic impulse—at one time jingoism was suggested; at another, pacificism. Taken as a whole, they are a most illuminating reflection of the confused spirit and temper of the time. In *The Dynasts* also, although the setting is that of the Napoleonic wars, we may discover an "occasional" tendency. Again the mental situation of the world at the opening of the new century is represented by the complexity of ideas and feelings exhibited in the dilemmas that one inevitably finds inherent in the work—the natural human passion and patriotic fervor of the poet—an Englishman in spite of himself—frequently run away with the wider, deeper, and more richly colored, but purely intellectual predetermined philosophical program. This is felt particularly in the Prologue and the Epilogue composed for the first public performance of parts of *The Dynasts* in 1914.

Another type of occasional poetry found in the Hardy-volumes is that of the lyric obituary. Mention has already been made of the poems written upon the death of Meredith, and of Swinburne, of Barnes, and of Hardy's own grandmother. To these might be added *The Abbey*

Mason, written in memory of his old architectural master, John Hicks of Dorchester, although it is merely a re-telling of an old legend and has no connection with Hicks other than its treatment of an architectural theme. But by far the most important, significant, and intrinsically valuable poetry of this kind is to be discovered in the *Poems of 1912-13.*

Late in 1912 Mrs. Hardy died most unexpectedly and after an extremely brief illness—"without ceremony," as the title of one of the poems expresses it. After the first shock of bereavement had spent its force, the poet proceeded to console himself by seeking refuge from the world of fact and retiring to the world of art, where his spirit might be refreshed by an indulgence in the untrammeled expression of its woes. The result was a series of poems that stand as his supreme achievement in the vein of pure lyric. Full of life, pity, and genuine feeling, they are more deeply and sincerely emotional, although more sober in tone, as a rule, than the purely imaginary situations elsewhere treated. Occasionally a particularly wistful or pathetic touch will recall the Wordsworth of the "Lucy" poems, but as a whole these *veteris vestigia flammae* are as distinctively individual as anything that this most individual poet has ever done. Without being logically connected together to form a symmetrical or compact unit, they present a fairly consistent record of a mood of bereavement, uncomforted by any hope of personal survival or reunion after death, but softened by reminiscences of past hours of blissful felicity.

The most imaginative of these poems, and the one that

The Lyric Poet (1898-1922)

exhibits the poet's "transcendental" tendencies in full-
est and richest fashion is *The Phantom Horsewoman,*
which shows also the great variety of the effects that the
remembrance of that memorable ride together, with
which the poet's mind seems obsessed, can produce. In
contrast to this is *The Spell of the Rose,* which, with its
perfectly transparent allegory, comes closest to an actual
record of events—the course of a domestic disagreement
and partial reconciliation is clearly suggested.

The most pathetic reflective piece is *Rain on a Grave,*
but an equally fine, though different, effect is achieved
by the coldest poem of the set, *A Circular,* which shows
admirably how pure thought can transfigure an ordinary
occurrence into real poetry:

> As "legal representative"
> I read a missive not my own,
> On new designs the senders give
> For clothes in tints as shown.
>
> Here figure blouses, gowns for tea,
> And presentation trains of state,
> Charming ball-dresses, millinery,
> Warranted up to date.
>
> And this gay-pictured, spring-time shout
> Of Fashion, hails what lady proud?
> Her who before last year ebbed out
> Was costumed in a shroud.

In strong contrast to the austerity and frigidity of
that, there is *The Voice,* as close an approach to a purely
emotional overflow as Hardy ever achieved, and for that

reason, perhaps, one of the most easily comprehensible of his poems.

> Woman much missed, how you call to me, call to me,
> Saying that now you are not as you were
> When you had changed from the one who was all to me,
> But as at first, when our day was fair.
>
> Can it be you that I hear? Let me view you, then,
> Standing as when I drew near to the town
> Where you would wait for me: yes, as I knew you then,
> Even to the original air-blue gown!
>
> Or is it only the breeze, in its listlessness
> Travelling across the wet mead to me here,
> Yet being ever dissolved to existlessness
> Heard no more again far or near?
>
> Thus I; faltering forward,
> Leaves around me falling,
> Wind oozing thin through the thorn from nor'ward,
> And the woman calling.

The effect of the whole series can not be reproduced by the citation of extracts and examples: the poems should be read, preferably at one sitting.

Hardy's special fields of interest,—all his "hobbies" —both artistic and scientific, can be traced as easily through his lyric poems as through his prose writings. If we now look into his poetry for expressions of his philosophical outlook upon human life and its significance in the general scheme of the universe, we shall find a most unexpected richness of material. Even without

The Lyric Poet (1898-1922)

taking into account *The Dynasts,* the avowed complete poetical and dramatic interpretation of the essentials of the Hardy world-view, we may discover in the philosophical lyrics a system of thought more complete, more consistent, and more compactly and pungently presented than in any or all of his novels. The essence of Hardy's thought and the centre of his artistic conceptions are, after all, a very general and universal conception of man's destiny rather than a minute picture of a strictly limited section of English countryside, which is developed merely as a vehicle for the presentation of something infinitely larger.

One aspect of the Hardy-viewpoint should be mentioned here, as it partially vindicates his claim to be regarded as a lyric poet. Great lyric poetry, according to Shelley, records "the happiest moments of the happiest souls." With this inspiring sentiment in mind, it is well to remember that there were times when Hardy felt an undeniable delight in life and that he frequently gives the lie to all his intellectual renunciative convictions. As he himself said, we are all "unreasoning, sanguine visionary." Not only did he "long to hold as truth what fancy saith," but he often could not help admitting that memory is better than oblivion, and Time, with all his tricks, preferable to no-time. His idealistic errantry overcame his cynicism, and he bravely followed his star. Even his conception of the Will admitted a hope that informing and merciful consciousness might come with the passage of the years, just as man's inhumanity to man may be overcome by the gradual rooting out of remediable evils—but the abiding love of life and of all that belongs to it, as expressed in the poem *Great Things,* remains his ultimate apology for producing lyric poetry:

Sweet cyder is a great thing,
 A great thing to me,
Spinning down to Weymouth town
 By Ridgeway thirstily,
And maid and mistress summoning
 Who tend the hostelry:
O cyder is a great thing,
 A great thing to me!

The dance is a great thing,
 A great thing to me,
With candles lit and partners fit
 For night-long revelry;
And going home when day-dawning
 Peeps pale upon the lea:
O dancing is a great thing,
 A great thing to me!

Love is, yea, a great thing,
 A great thing to me,
When, having drawn across the dawn
 In darkness silently,
A figure flits, like one a-wing
 Out from the nearest tree:
O love is, yes, a great thing,
 Aye, greatest thing to me!

Will these be always great things,
 Greatest things to me? . . .
Let it befall that One will call,
 "Soul, I have need of thee":

The Lyric Poet (1898-1922)

What then? Joy-jaunts, impassioned flings,
  Love, and its ecstasy,
Will always have been great things,
  Greatest things to me!

      *   *

     *

Until recently, the poetry of Thomas Hardy has been very generally ignored, and when noticed at all, usually vastly underestimated. Ardent propagandists have been arising of late, however, and at present some of the ablest critics have shown themselves as eager champions of the veteran poet. William Archer, Edmund Gosse, and Clement Shorter formed a triumvirate of whole-hearted admirers from the start, in 1898. Alfred Noyes grew very enthusiastic over *The Dynasts* and the later lyrics, while Max Beerbohm, for all his flippant manner, failed to hide a considerable admiration for the great "Epic-Drama." In the United States two of the most distinguished of the newer poets have joined in regarding Hardy as the only Englishman with any real claim to be considered a great figure in the world of poetry. They are Edwin Arlington Robinson, the representative of the more austere and restrained style of contemporary poetic composition, and John Gould Fletcher, one of the "Imagist" leaders, who has written this of Hardy:

He has illustrated his vision to the world by writing poetry so beautiful, so weighty with idea and expression, that to turn to it from the rhymes of the Georgians, or from the vers-libristic efforts of more futuristic singers, is like turning to Bach or Beethoven from the efforts of a rag-time band.

[217]

The Life of Thomas Hardy

It is rather remarkable to find such praise from an avowed modernist and iconoclast bestowed upon a writer whose early work drew the admiration of Tennyson and Stevenson. Time has never outstripped Mr. Hardy to leave him behind as an interesting but valueless relic of a past generation. Beginning with some faint traces of the school of Tennyson, he quickly managed to forge his way out of Victorianism, nor did he succumb to the seductive but cloying strains of the "fleshly school," nor was he carried away by the revived mediævalism of the latter part of the century. Bridging a dangerous period of doubtful taste with his attention concentrated on his fiction, he developed independently an uncompromising terseness and swiftness of poetic language, coupled with an imaginative fire and pungency of thought that carries his latest work along in the van of modern poetry. His verse has its roots far back in the Romantic revolt of the early years of the Nineteenth Century and in the rediscovery of the lyric and dramatic ecstasy of the Elizabethans—and its branches embrace the latest discoveries and developments of the Twentieth Century renaissance, particularly that of the younger group of American poets, and they extend at times far into the future of the art. As has been pointed out before, he is at once the oldest and the youngest of our poets.

Whether or not the world of to-day will be found justified in showing itself far more grateful for Thomas Hardy's novels than for his poems, there is no doubt about his own opinion in the matter: in his poetry he has consummated his earliest and latest literary ambition. General opinion agrees with Dr. William Lyon Phelps,

Thomas Hardy, O. M. (1913). From a
photograph by Bernard Griffin, Dorchester.

who, in commenting on the seeming strangeness of the judgments of authors about their own work, remarks: "Thomas Hardy firmly believes that his poems are much greater than *The Return of the Native* and *Tess of the D'Urbervilles*. But I do not care what he thinks so long as we have his masterpieces of fiction." One cannot dispute what is perhaps a question of personal taste, but on the other hand statements like the following, continually encountered among those to whom Hardy's poems are still a novelty, are calculated to raise the ire of those whose judgments agree with Hardy's own:

> Mr. Hardy is a novelist who remains a novelist, more or less, in his verse; there is always drama lurking in it somewhere. He very rarely, one concludes, writes verse from any strong lyrical impulse, though now and then there are beautiful and surprising lyrical touches. . . . Meredith—to whom Mr. Hardy pays a noble tribute in this volume (*Time's Laughingstocks*)—was essentially and almost primarily a poet; to Mr. Hardy the verse form is rather experimental than inevitable.

It is hardly necessary to point out or comment on the perfectly absurd mixing up of literary genera in the first sentence of the foregoing criticism; and Meredith and Hardy, so different in spirit, the one representing the comic tradition running back through the third Earl of Shaftesbury, the other reaching back through the pure tragic tradition of *Othello* and *Prometheus Bound,* can hardly be compared as to the quality of their poetry.

Over against this sort of high-handed depreciation of Hardy's poetry, which may sometimes be partly due to over-enthusiastic appreciation of his fiction, one finds

The Life of Thomas Hardy

with surprise the exact reverse of such judgment coming from Coventry Patmore, who, as early as March 29th, 1875, wrote to Hardy to express his regret that "such almost unequalled beauty and power as appeared in the novels should not have assured themselves the immortality which would have been conferred upon them by the form of verse."

Without attempting a dogmatic opinion on a matter which will be decided by future generations, if at all, one may perhaps with a show of reason point out a possible analogy between the form assumed by the bulk of Mr. Hardy's productions and by Goethe's works. Both created transcendent novels and remarkable lyrical poems, but concentrated the sustained efforts of many years upon the production of one great piece of cosmic poetry; —in the one case *Faust* was the result, in the other *The Dynasts*. Without following out the analogy too closely or attempting to judge the final relative merit of the two poets, perhaps impossible at present, we may possibly be aided somewhat in our attempted estimate of the relative importance of the works of Hardy by observing the manner in which posterity has rated those of Goethe.

CHAPTER IX

The Cosmic Poet (1903-1908)

*T*HE opening years of the present century witnessed the fulfilment of a project that had long been in the stage of fermentation in Hardy's mind. For many years he had quietly nursed the ambition of presenting an epic treatment of the Napoleonic conflict that should adequately show England's share in that struggle against the world-tyranny of an autocratic military genius. But, exercising that restraint which is so characteristic of genius, he deferred the execution of this plan until he had won at least some recognition as a poet with his first two volumes of verse. Two years after *Poems of the Past and the Present* had been launched against a world of readers still sceptical of the poet's powers and equipment, appeared Part One of *The Dynasts*. The title had been chosen from a phrase out of the Magnificat, which is echoed in the final chorus of Pities in Part III: "Who hurlest Dynasts from their thrones." A footnote gives the Greek of the original: "*καθετλε* ΔΥΝΑΣΤΑΣ *ἀπὸ θρόνων.*"

Much as Hardy's late turn to poetry had surprised his readers, no one was prepared to receive this stupendous torso in 1903 without feeling profound astonishment at the resourcefulness, daring or imbecility of the veteran author—particularly as the title-page announced that

[221]

the completed work would consist of "three parts, nineteen acts, and one hundred and forty scenes." Such gigantic proportions were unexpected in the declining years of even such a giant as Thomas Hardy. The preface, the list of characters, the dramatic form, the supernatural machinery, and, above all, the portentous opening:

What of the Immanent Will and its designs?

were calculated to fill the gentle reader with nothing short of consternation and dismay—and they did; they still do. Reviewers very seldom got beyond expressions of petulant amazement before the ends of their articles. They scarcely recovered in time to notice the delightful scenes on the Wessex coast and the glorious depiction of Trafalgar, so absorbed were they in the provokingly philosophical "anatomy of the Immanent Will."

Part II, dealing with Napoleon's successful continental campaigns and with the English victories in the Peninsula, followed in 1906; and Part III, concerned with the disasters of Moscow and Waterloo, completed the trilogy in 1908. By this time the more discriminating readers and the less prejudiced critics had begun to discern signs of real greatness in the work. It was seen to be a *magnum opus* and not a monstrosity. Although it has received extravagant praise since then, sometimes from authorities of eminence, it is still comparatively unknown.

It is interesting to note the gradual conversion of its critics from frank hostility to warm approval and some measure of enthusiasm. When Part I appeared, there

The Cosmic Poet (1903-1908)

was, as Alfred Noyes put it, "a general disposition
among critics to 'hum' and 'ha.'" "The furtive yelp
of the masked and writhing poeticule"—as another Victorian poet exuberantly described it—"did not fail, however, to testify to the real greatness of the strange in-
truder." The change in the attitude of reviewers from
disapprobation and dismay at the immense proportions,
the mighty themes, and the iconoclastic methods of the
work, to sympathy and understanding, draws the attention of the investigator immediately. In the London *Nation*, for instance, the review of the first part was frankly
hostile. Mr. Hardy was brusquely ordered to return
to novel-writing—being definitely pigeonholed in which
field, presumably, he would be powerless to annoy the
critic with fresh demands upon the intellect or imagination. The remarks which appeared in the same periodi-
cal after the publication of the third part, are worth re-
peating as an admirable summary of the course of critical opinion during the four years which intervened between the publication of the first and last sections.

Four years ago we gave a dazed and tentative notice to the
first part of Thomas Hardy's huge closet drama. . . . As a
whole it seemed to us as a *succes manqué,* a piece of imaginative
incunabula, the characteristic product of a moody, or, as Mr.
Hardy calls it, a "nervous and quizzical age," a product which
might some day, in an age of stronger artistic feeling, be made
by another hand the basis of a masterpiece. On the appearance
of the second part, two years later, we found ourselves still more
deeply impressed with the things that were striking in the first
part. Now, with the publication of the third and last part, that
suspicion has become a certainty. We have read the final volume
with the complete absorption of every faculty, and going back

[223]

The Life of Thomas Hardy

from it to read again the first and second parts, with the original preface wherein the plan of the whole was laid down, we have become aware of a work marked, despite its superficial uncouthness, by a colossal unity and a staggering significance—a climax of that long series of novels in which Mr. Hardy has embodied both his poignant knowledge of the world of men and his grim, undeluded philosophy.

The elements composing this masterwork had been developing in the mind of the author for a long time. As early as June 20, 1875, we find that he entered in his notebook the suggestion that he might attempt "An Iliad of Europe from 1789 to 1815." Five years later we find him writing *The Trumpet-Major,* in which he used the grim background of the war as an effective foil to the gay and mellow portrayal of an idyllic but pathetic lovestory. Here we find such martial touches as the great review of King George's legions on the Wessex Downs, the false alarm of Bonaparte's invasion of the island, and the glorious news of Trafalgar. Especially interesting and effective is the introduction of the author's kinsman, Sir Thomas Masterman Hardy, as a character into the story. All these influences excite and move the unimportant and peaceful country people "as a groundswell moves the weeds in a cave." Among the shorter tales that were written during the latter part of his fiction period, there are several that bear testimony to the increasing insistence with which this favorite theme cried for expression. *A Committee-Man of "The Terror"* deals with the earlier French Revolution, with the action taking place in England; *The Melancholy Hussar of the German Legion* is a tragic tale of the *Heimweh*

The Cosmic Poet (1903-1908)

of George's foreign troops; and *A Tradition of 1804,* told in dialect by old Solomon Selby, a one-time smuggler, recounts the actual landing of "Boney," "the Corsican ogre," in the night with a French officer, to discover a suitable place on the Wessex coast for the landing of his army of invasion.

Parallel to this gradual development of interest in the subject, and, one may reasonably suppose, the accumulation of a great amount of historical and legendary material, there developed in the poet's mind a conception of history—indeed of all human activity—as the manifestation of one mysterious immanent causality, which is finally termed "Will." This philosophical concept is made the intellectual basis by which the historical events are interpreted, and is invested with a lyric and dramatic machinery of its own.

Why Hardy chose the form of a gigantic poetic drama instead of that of the historical romance or of the epic poem is a question that the critic must answer as best he can. The best point of departure for a discussion of Hardy in his new rôle of dramatist is undoubtedly the set of his own opinions delivered to the *Pall Mall Gazette* in August, 1892. William Archer in an article in the *Fortnightly Review* had urged the desirability of a reunion between literature and the drama; had suggested that living novelists were to blame for the poor quality of the writing for the stage of the time, and that they owed it to themselves and to literature to make some essay in dramatic form. Thereupon the *Pall Mall Gazette* invited the leading novelists to answer these questions:

The Life of Thomas Hardy

1. Whether you regard the present divorce of fiction from the drama as beneficial or inimical to the best interests of literature and the stage;

2. Whether you, yourself, have at any time had, or now have, any desire to exercise your gifts in the production of plays as well as of novels; and, if not,

3. Why you consider the novel the better or more convenient means of bringing your ideas before the public you address.

Hardy's reply reads as follows:

1. Inimical to the best interests of the stage: no injury to literature.

2. Have occasionally had a desire to produce a play, and have, in fact, written the skeletons of several. Have no such desire in any special sense just now.

3. Because, in general, the novel affords scope for getting nearer to the heart and meaning of things than does the play: in particular the play as nowadays conditioned, when parts have to be moulded to actors, not actors to parts; when managers will not risk a truly original play; when scenes have to be arranged in a constrained and arbitrary fashion to suit the exigencies of stage-building, although spectators are absolutely indifferent to order and succession, provided they can have set before them a developing thread of interest. The reason of this arbitrary arrangement would seem to be that the presentation of human passions is subordinated to the presentation of mountains, cities, clothes, furniture, plate, jewels, and other real and sham-real appurtenances, to the neglect of the principle that the material stage should be a conventional or figurative arena, in which accessories are kept down to the plane of mere suggestion of place and time, so as not to interfere with the high-relief of the action and emotions.

To the student of *The Dynasts* this is very interesting. Hardy betrayed here a real interest in the drama and

Forescene.

The Overworld

Enter the Spirit & Chorus of the Years, the Spirit & Chorus of the Pities, the Spirit of the Earth, the Spirits Sinister & Ironic with their Choruses ~~Chorus of Sinister Spirits~~, minor Spirits, Spirit-messengers & Recording Angels.

Spirit of the Earth

What of the Immanent Will & Its designs?

Spirit of the Years.

It works unconsciously, as heretofore,
Eternal artistries in Circumstance,
Whose patterns, planned by rapt aesthetic rote,
Seem in themselves Its single listless aim,
And not their consequence.

Chorus of the Pities (aerial music.)

Still thus? Still thus? ~~Still thus?~~
~~Ear age~~ Ever unconscious!
An automatic sense ¶ unweeting why or whence?
Then be Its inevitable, as of old,
Although that so it be we dare not hold!

A page from the manuscript of *The Dynasts*. Reproduced through the courtesy of the British Museum.

The Cosmic Poet (1903-1908)

asserted that he had made occasional essays in the form. The field was not new to him, then. Of the many dramatizations of the novels he was probably responsible for at least one, *The Three Wayfarers,* a one-act pastoral play adapted from *The Three Strangers,* in *Wessex Tales.* What he objected to was the restriction imposed upon the dramatist by the external demands of the stage-technique of the day. The writing of *The Dynasts* showed no deviation from the principles here enunciated. No reliance was placed upon the powers of stage-craft to reproduce the desired setting; the imagination of the reader was assumed to be able to cope with the problem of adequate visualization of the scenes.

Even before the publication and actual production of *The Dynasts,* Hardy's dramatic talents occasionally revealed themselves. Commentators on the novels noted that the Wessex countrymen often played the part of chorus to the tragedy enacted. This was felt particularly in such a book as *The Return of the Native,* where the rustics not only assemble for their quasi-pagan bonfire festival and introduce the audience to the atmosphere and characters of the story to come, but also indulge in a wild sort of choric dance. Likewise Aunt Drusilla in *Jude* is essentially a chorus-figure in her comments on the action. The author prefixed a list of *dramatis personæ* to *A Pair of Blue Eyes,* and the essential "dramatic unities" were observed in nearly all of the greater prose-tragedies.

In certain of the lyric poems also, we can detect a strong predilection for the drama. Hardy's liking for the dramatic monologue has already been touched upon.

The Life of Thomas Hardy

Friends Beyond with its ghostly but nevertheless very human characters, and *Winter in Durnover Field,* with its bird-speakers, are delightful essays in the form of the lyric "mime." The lure of the stage is the prime motive of the action of *The Noble Lady's Tale.* It is possible then, to assert with some show of reason that Hardy was not a bungling and untried novice in the field of the drama, even though he did not at first intend ever to have *The Dynasts* actually presented before an audience, even in part.

Nothing exactly like *The Dynasts* in form has ever been written before. Any analysis of the work, no matter from what point of view, must take cognizance of the fact that, as it stands, it is a unification of two great themes, the War and the Will,—and that this dualism in idea or content has caused a corresponding dualism in form, machinery, and even expression. First there is the human story—the historical drama—with its human agents, motives, and actions, playing upon the stage of Europe. Surrounding and permeating this clash of peoples and ideals there is the philosophical action, with its machinery of allegorical figures, playing in an "Overworld," in the unlimited universe of pure Idea. The first element in the Epic-Drama finds expression in the dialect, prose, or blank verse of the human actors and in the Hardyan prose of the stage-directions and "dumb shows"; the second element is presented through exceedingly various types of lyric measures, punctuated occasionally by the "familiar" prose of the Spirit Ironic. The *dramatis personæ* of the terrestrial action consist of kings, princes, councillors, generals, admirals, armies,

The Cosmic Poet (1903-1908)

common people, messengers, mobs,—humanity in all its aspects; the supernatural actors are the Ancient Spirit of the Years, the Shade of the Earth, the Spirit of the Pities, the Spirits Sinister and Ironic, spirit messengers, rumors, and recording angels, and choruses of the Years, Pities, and Sinister and Ironic spirits. The resources of typography are employed to make clear to the reader the difference in atmosphere. The poetry declaimed by the spirits is italicized, the dialogue of mortals is printed in the ordinary open-face type, and the stage-directions for both the actions is in small type, which frequently produces a very real and significant effect of uncanny aloofness, as when we are told that the peals of bells are heard faintly by the supernatural spectators. The point of view of the audience, or reader, which is usually also that of the spirits as well, is shifted about with complete freedom. The action of the humans is observed from the most convenient point, whether that be close to the scene, or so far on high that all of Europe can be taken in at a glance.

Even as Homer's gods often intermingled with the mortal heroes in their struggles, so do Hardy's abstractions occasionally interfere with the human action, usually causing some little annoyance to the reader if he is logical-minded. It is indeed in the welding together or in the combination of the two actions or viewpoints in the book that the greatest difficulties are encountered. Mr. Gosse, and many a critic after him, found it hard at times to reconcile the attitude towards life expressed by the spirits (reminding him of the refrain of a popular coster-song: "What's the use of anythink?" "Why, nothink!'') with the motivation of the mortal characters according to the dictates of the doctrine of complete free-will.

The particular "Epic-Drama" form of *The Dynasts* is an original invention with Hardy; yet, before hitting upon it, he must have consciously or unconsciously been influenced by a number of somewhat similar literary monuments produced by great cosmic poets before him. Perhaps his favorite *Book of Job* suggested something of the idea of having celestial machinery to surround and to account for the course of human events; perhaps the Shakespearean "Histories" fired his ambitions to present England's heroes in the poetical drama of action; perhaps the angelic choruses of Goethe's *Faust* had something to do with his conception of commenting choruses of spiritual essences and chanting recording angels; perhaps the *Prometheus Unbound* of Shelley influenced both the form and the "irreconcilable" content of the work. All of these literary progenitors, in fact, can be made to present remarkable similarities in point of view and subject matter in the realm of pure idea, as well as in form and structure, and it is perhaps in conjunction with another work, such as one of these, similar in scope, power and imagination, that the characteristics of *The Dynasts* can be best studied. None of the works mentioned, however, can vie with the tragedies of Æschylus in the richness of comparative material presented. It would be hard to find two poets, produced by two entirely different civilizations, so closely allied in the problems they choose for treatment and in their manner of treating them, as the Æschylus of Eleusis,

The Cosmic Poet (1903-1908)

Greece, of 460 B.C., and the Thomas Hardy of Dorchester, England, of 1910.

In a previous chapter we have observed how Hardy's enthusiasm and sympathy for the work of the classical tragedians made itself felt throughout his career, and in spite of his avowed repudiation of what he considers the Greek optimism, that "revelling in the general situation." The work of no other English writer of the past generation has so frequently invoked comparison with the ideals of Æschylean tragedy as his. W. S. Durrant, for instance, has pointed out striking and elaborate parallelisms between *Jude the Obscure* and the work of Æschylus. With reference to the novels only, he says: "To put it briefly, Mr. Hardy is the modern exponent of the guiding principles of ancient Greek tragedy," and he speaks of *Jude the Obscure* as "nothing less than the product of an intellectual *avatar,* for surely when the story was conceived, the spirit of Æschylus lived again in Thomas Hardy. Nowhere in the ancient tragedies of the great master is Destiny more relentless in pursuing its victim than in this most modern of tragedies cast in the form of prose narrative." Professor Cunliffe, in writing of *The Return of the Native,* declares that "Hardy's ideal of literary art is Greek tragedy, and it is an ideal with which, in spite of obvious differences, he has much in common."

It is worth noting, that just as the plays of Æschylus can be said to have been born of the Persian wars, so did Hardy look to the historical and legendary past of his nation for material with which to clothe his ideas. *The Persians* of Æschylus, therefore, which actually celebrated the early victory of western over eastern civilization in wondrous fashion, may form the subject of a close comparison with *The Dynasts,* which aimed to celebrate a democratic British victory over the imperialism of Napoleon. But of still greater interest than this comparison, which will be treated in detail in the sequel, is the similarity of the great problems with which both writers were primarily concerned. The late Professor Wheeler, in summing up the inner subject matter of the Greek tragedians, has used expressions which might very well have been written by a reviewer of *The Dynasts:*

> The Greek tragic poets were earnest students of the problems and mysteries of human life. Man's relation to the universe about him, his obligation to the unseen powers which control the universe, his duties to his fellow-beings, the seeming conflicts between human and divine law, all these form the material of the Greek tragedy.

Thomas Hardy as well as Æschylus brooded on the mysteries of life and the world, the general riddle of existence, and the validity of the moral law; and it is striking that after a lapse of twenty-four centuries a work appears similar to an ancient predecessor not only in the treatment of these ideas, but even in the terrestrial and celestial machinery employed for the outward clothing of the problems. When we think of the personified spiritual essences invoked by Hardy and governing his great panoramic show, continually making their presence and influence felt in the action of the human puppets below, we are elevated to the sphere of Æschylus' sublime imagination, where the elemental forces of the universe seem close about us. Both authors dwell among the clouds and, like Socrates, are at home there. Both are actuated by the keenest pity for the wretchedness of human life, and by an overwhelming fear of the unknown and unknowable—the two governing motives of all that is best in tragedy, according to Aristotle. Hardy represents the culmination of an age of scepticism and of the storm and stress of religious doubt, analogous to the age which immediately followed the generation of Æschylus in Greece and was represented by the critical attitude assumed by Euripides in matters of orthodox pagan beliefs. Such an age almost invariably follows a conventionally "romantic" one. Hardy follows Æschylus in sequence of ideas much more naturally than one would expect, considering the lapse of so many centuries.

The very real closeness of Thomas Hardy to the classical ideal in dealing with an epic subject can be observed in the fact that he centers his attention on broad questions of Destiny and Collective Will, viewing individual human suffering sympathetically, but as no more than a by-product. This is an attitude frequently found in classical writers and not always perfectly understood by modern readers. In the *Trachinian Women* of Sophocles, for instance, one cannot fail to be struck by Heracles' lack of forgiveness for Deianeira and his utter disregard for her feelings, but we may be certain that the members of the Athenian audience did not notice this, with their attention centred in the divine mission of the hero. Likewise in the *Æneid*, Dido's tragic end, so disturbing to modern notions of the ideal relations between hero and heroine, was probably dwarfed immeasurably in the eyes

of the Roman readers by the main consideration of
Æneas's fulfilment of Rome's destiny. In like manner
when reading *The Dynasts* one is conscious of the chill-
ing effect which the dominant conception of the Immanent Will has upon the purely human motives introduced
into the play. This combination of a typically classical
viewpoint with an occasional modern exploitation of sentiment forms indeed one of the outstanding excellences
of the work, although the superficial reader may feel it
as a dilemma. While Hardy expresses his view of life
consciously, definitely, and frankly, Æschylus works
more unconsciously and does not force his intellectual
convictions to the surface, leaving them rather to be naturally reflected or implied in his work. In this respect
the ancient writer is the greater poet.

Hardy and Æschylus are strikingly alike in the way
they regard and treat the language they use—and this
in spite of the fact that they use widely different languages. Both apply with the greatest freedom the principle of the essential flexibility and fluidity of language.
The opinion of the conservative contemporaries of
Æschylus as to the language he employed is very amus-
ingly presented in the famous scene of the contest of
words between the shades of Euripides and of Æschylus
in Aristophanes' *Frogs*. The method of weighing in a
balance single lines of the rival authors is employed in
order to determine which of the two writes the weightier
verse. Æschylus, of course, is the easy winner—his re-
sounding phrases never fail to send the carefully
wrought lines of his younger rival soaring upward. It
would be interesting to apply the same comparative test,

The Life of Thomas Hardy

The general formal plan of *The Dynasts* has a distinct
family relationship with that of Greek tragedy. As a
trilogy it bears the same sort of resemblance to the classical form that a full-grown lion bears to a kitten. There
is in it the same unity of theme and treatment, although
greatly enlarged and complicated. Each part is complete
in itself, like the separate Greek plays, and yet all three
are indissolubly bound together by the absolute identity
of the underlying theme and the philosophical background. Here Hardy is much closer to Æschylus than
to either Sophocles or Euripides, because the elder
dramatist felt the trilogy, and not the single play, as the
essential dramatic unit. Nearly all the puzzling critical
problems with which the *Prometheus Bound* is surrounded, and all the misconceptions which have grown
up with regard to its ultimate ethical significance, would
almost certainly be cleared up if its two companion-plays
had come down to us. As the play stands, it is dramatically a small formal unit, but ethically a headless torso.
It presents to the audience a truly remarkable πλοκή,
or complication, but hardly a shadow of a λύσις, or
solution. As tragedy developed after Æschylus, as the
importance of the chorus was diminished, as plays became longer because of the extra time thus given for the
spoken dialogue itself, and as realism gradually crept in,
the single play became the unit, and we find Euripides
writing three almost independent plays. Æschylus might
be said to have produced three-act tragedies; Euripides,
cycles of loosely-connected one-act "social dramas." In
its general form *The Dynasts* is Æschylean, while the
works of Ibsen and of the manufacturers of the "well-

made play'' are essentially Euripidean. It may remind the reader of the Shakespearean ''chronicle-history'' type—but ''histories,'' from the lost *Fall of Miletus* on (which, according to Herodotus, caused an audience of Athenians to burst into tears), could nearly all come under the general heading of ''tragedy.'' Hardy is closer to the Greeks than to modern writers in his lavish use of spectacle. The serious plays of to-day very rarely beguile their audiences with processions, pageants, armies, courts, or battles, but of these things the Greeks were very fond. They were naturally suggested also by the peculiar conditions of the vast open-air Dyonysiac theatre, built into the side of the Acropolis, and by the necessary processional entrance, choral evolutions, and exit of a large and stately chorus.

The function of the chorus when employed in a drama has never materially changed since the time of Æschylus. It has been called ''the spectator idealized,'' but its greatest value, from the playwright's point of view, is that it enables him to reach the audience directly, and to permit the characters he has created to remain themselves. It is the instrument by which the dramatist relays what he considers to be the correct emotional or intellectual reaction to the audience. In *The Dynasts* the actors themselves merely act—they do not express the author's opinions, and the drama itself gains immensely in force thereby. The very individual interpretation of the significance of history is expressed solely through the ''phantom intelligences'' and their choruses.

Henry Newbolt has emphasized the differences between the choruses of *The Dynasts* and the Greek chorus as definitely as they can be articulated at all. He points out that the "phantom intelligences" are not visibly embodied in the play, and are therefore unconditioned by it; and that the Greek chorus, as the spectator idealized, represents either the national spirit or the universal sympathy of human nature, whereas the choruses in *The Dynasts* represent the author alone, and his personal philosophy. It may also be claimed that Hardy's "Pities," "Years," and "Rumors" partake more of the character of the personified abstractions of the later mediæval morality-plays than of the comparatively real persons of the Greek chorus. However, this is only partially true. That the representation of abstract qualities was not totally unknown, even in rather early Hellenic times, can be seen in the opening of the *Prometheus,* in which the unwilling Hephæstus is urged on to the ugly task of chaining the Titan to the rocks by the demons "Strength" and "Force."

Comparison of the various species of supernatural intelligences in *The Dynasts* with similar choruses in the extant work of Æschylus leads to interesting results. There is a remarkable parallelism between Hardy's "Pities" and the chorus of Ocean Nymphs in the *Prometheus,* who, because of their sympathy with the suffering Titan, voluntarily suffer all his agonies with him. Both choruses are distinguished by an incomparable beauty of conception. Both are composed of minor divinities in their authors' pantheons, and are intensely human in their feelings. With their essentially tender natures subjected to a heartrending strain, they display an unconquerable loyalty to ideals, although such loyalty involves,

The history of the drama shows that there is almost no limit to the imagination of an audience, if properly coaxed, in supplying the deficiencies of the theatre. Let us consider for a moment the stage-problem which the *Prometheus* must have presented in its day. The scene is a gigantic cleft or rock in the most desolate part of Scythia. Against this rock the Titan is suspended, nailed and bound in "indissoluble fetters of adamantine bonds." Later come the winged ocean nymphs, Oceanus himself, with his car drawn by hippogriffs, the mad heifer-maiden Io, and finally the god Hermes. Realistic presentation of such scenes is manifestly impossible, even to-day. How it was managed in the crude theatre of Æschylus must remain a source of conjecture. It is obviously a futile thing, then, to condemn the dramatic form of *The Dynasts* on the grounds of its impossibility as a stage-play. No play can be given with complete realism, and it is a difficult thing to set a definite limit beyond which the author must not tax the imagination. Neither the *Prometheus* nor the *Eumenides,* nor the *Dynasts* is a real stage-play, yet all of these have been acted with success, winning their audience by means of their inherent dramatic power and effectiveness. The Greeks did not seem to mind the fact that in the *Prometheus* the rock was possibly represented by some kind of wicker-work and Prometheus himself by a huge dummy, as has been conjectured, and the London audiences seem to have accepted gladly Granville Barker's ingenious conventional representation of the many dramatic "absurdities" of *The Dynasts*. Aristotle, with whom it is always a pleasure to agree in such things, has himself said that the

The Cosmic Poet (1903-1908)

power of tragedy should be felt apart from representation and actors.

The production of *The Dynasts* in abbreviated form at the Kingsway Theatre, London, on November 25, 1914, forms a rather unique paragraph in English stage history. It is the story of an unplayable play made playable. Hardy had already tentatively suggested in the Preface, that a performance some day might be made possible by the use of a "monotonic delivery of speeches, with dreamy conventional gestures, something in the manner traditionally maintained by the old Christmas mummers . . . with gauzes or screens to blur the outlines . . . and shut off the actual." This suggestion despite the rather apologetic manner in which it was thrown out, drew a small storm of ridicule from the reviewers, as might have been expected. Yet the actual performance proved "a success no less delightful than unlikely." A special prologue and epilogue were added by Hardy for this performance. The prologue is as follows:

> In these stern times of ours, when crimson strife
> Throws shade on every thoroughfare of life,
> Disfigures comely countries with its gore,
> And sends back mangled heroes to our shore,
> The gift of gifts is sturdy hardihood,
> That holds it firm through each vicissitude,
> Not only hour by hour, but year by year,
> If need be, till life's lurid skies be clear.
> Arrested by perceptions such as this
> We gather that it may not be amiss,—
> During the few brief minutes you can spare,
> From the innumerable claims that call your care

To raise up visions of historic ware
Which taxed the endurance of our ancestors;
That such reminders of the feats they did
May stouten hearts now strained by issues hid;
Therefore we have essayed to represent,
By our faint means, event upon event
That Europe saw a hundred years ago—
—What matters that Napoleon was our foe?
Fair France herself had no ambitious ends;
And we are happy in a change that tends
To make the nearest neighbours closest friends.

This is the epilogue:

May such reminders soon forever pass,
And war be but a shade on memory's glass,
And might uphold the injured people's cause,
And Europe move again to genial laws;
May soon succumb all influences malign,
And still the Star of England proudly shine!
                                    God save the King!

The prose commentary was assigned to a reader, and such lyric passages as were retained were delivered by two stately "muses." It is interesting thus to find the most feasible way of dealing with the chorus-matter to be by means of the Elizabethan induction machinery. The stage itself was also handled in Elizabethan fashion, with an inner stage for "scenes," while only properties were used on the main stage. What this performance chiefly served to bring out, besides the possibility of presenting the poem on the stage at all, was the intense dramatic quality of the scenes. At the same time, this production did not attempt, nor did it achieve, the impossible. The inevitable shortcoming of any conceivable possible performance of *The Dynasts* is the manifest impossibility to do adequate justice to the remarkable expression of the author's philosophy as found in the work. Nearly all of the passages recited by the muses are reported to have been taken from the sections allotted to the "Pities." Although we can imagine the effect of this procedure to have been very satisfactory, the probability is that the poem suffered a total loss of the great spiritual conflict presented by the supernatural creations of the author, which in the reading overshadows and dominates the whole of the terrestrial action. We are told in the poem that the speech of mortals should sound rather thin when heard in comparison with the chantings of the divinities. In a production where, we are told, the "Immanent Will" is hardly mentioned at all, and then only near the close, the loss of philosophical unity must have been considerable. "The vast sweep of the poem," Mr. Harold Child says, "its poetic unity, its infinite variety, its mystery and majesty, in fact all the bigness of it —these were lost. The proportions were destroyed. Man became huge and the heavens were tucked away in corners."

Scenic impossibilities have been overcome by both Æschylus and Thomas Hardy by the simplest of all means, the use of description. When the ancient dramatist cannot have the scene he wishes placed before the physical eye of his audience, he presents it to the mind's eye by letting one of the *dramatis personæ* describe it. This is true of the description of the setting of the *Prometheus,* and of the Battle of Salamis, which is reported by messenger in *The Persians*. Hardy's manner of portraying battles is essentially the same, except that he lets the stage directions or "dumb show" tell the story which the Athenians would have heard narrated by the messenger. In both dramatists these descriptions are intensely vivid and effective. In *The Dynasts* there is nothing which surpasses the following passage, dealing with the close of the Battle of Waterloo:

> The reds disappear from the sky, and the dusk grows deeper. The action of the battle degenerates into a hunt, and recedes further and further into the distance southward. When the tramplings and shouts of the combatants have dwindled, the lower sounds are noticeable that come from the wounded: hopeless appeals, cries for water, elaborate blasphemies, and impotent execrations of Heaven and hell. In the vast and dusky shambles black slouching shapes begin to move, the plunderers of the dead and dying.
>
> The night grows clear and beautiful, and the moon shines musingly down. But instead of the sweet smell of green herbs and dewy rye as at her last shining upon these fields, there is now the stench of gunpowder and a muddy stew of crushed crops and gore.

Who could wish to exchange this terrible and pitiful picture for even the most beautiful stage-set that can be contrived? The reader is reminded of a few lines in *The Persians* whose similarity, in idea and expression, to the close of many of Hardy's battle-scenes is unmistakable. Both poets seem to have been acutely affected by the mingled horror and beauty of a moonlight night following a battle. The very words of Æschylus cannot fail to associate the two authors together immediately:

Hardy receiving the degree of D. Litt. at Oxford. To his right is Mrs. Hardy; to his left, Lady Raleigh, wife of Sir Walter Raleigh, late Professor of English Literature at the University.

The Cosmic Poet (1903-1908)

... οἰμωγὴ δ' ὁμοῦ
κωκύμασιν κατεῖχε πελαγίαν ἅλα,
ἕως κελαινῆς νυκτὸς ὄμμ' ἀφειλέτο.

It has already been mentioned that the main sources of inspiration for both writers were similar—that they both looked to the immediate historical past of their nations and found there a chronicle of glorious deeds worthy to be immortalized. Both poets wrote from the standpoint of the winning side and both believed they were recording the defeat of a vaunting and unjustified despotism. With all their intense nationalism, however, neither of them failed to be actuated at times with the keenest pity for their fallen or vanquished enemies. In *The Persians* the note of triumph of the Greeks is almost completely submerged in the pity and horror at the misfortunes of the oriental nation. The essential identity, both of intention and of effect achieved by both writers can be best observed in a comparison of the wonderfully vivid and gripping description of the Battle of Salamis in *The Persians* with Hardy's justly admired picture of the Battle of Trafalgar, in which the progress of the struggle is told in the "stage-directions" or the "dumb show." Striking superficial similarities are not lacking. Both battles show the victory of a small but compactly organized and trained naval force of a single nation over a large and unwieldy combination of ships of various nationalities. The Greeks and the English are both inflamed with a fervent patriotism and love of the democratic institutions they defend—and this spirit is in both cases represented as inspiring every man, from the ad-

[245]

miral to the cabin-boys. Both poets also use the great
national watchwords and battlecries, Hardy quoting with
great effect Nelson's famous signals to his fleet, and
Æschylus putting lines into the mouth of the messenger
that must have drawn out all the enthusiasm the Athenians were capable of expressing on the occasion of their
solemn dramatic and religious festival. Opposed to the
small, confident, and high-spirited bodies we see in the
one case the imperfect amalgam of French and Spanish
units, under the leadership of the tragically hopeless and
vacillating Admiral Villeneuve, and in the other, the vast
conglomeration of Persian and countless other barbarian
vessels arrayed in all their exotic and decadent splendor.
In the portrayal of the losing side in both instances, we
receive a vision of oriental power, pomp, and magnifi-
cence, touched with a characteristically oriental note of
sadness and fatalism. Although there was as little doubt
as to the outcome in the minds of the Greek audience as
there is to modern readers of *The Dynasts*, yet the sus-
pense is admirably sustained by both poets, and the
parallel scenes can be read again and again, and retain
their fascination undiminished.

Heroic characters in *The Dynasts* and in Æschylean
tragedy present a series of most interesting Plutarchian
studies and comparisons. Napoleon, as the great central
figure of the modern epic-drama demands our first attention, although Mr. Abercrombie makes the very sugges-
tive observation that the whole Napoleonic chronicle oc-
cupies a position in Thomas Hardy's work analogous to
that of the single character of Prometheus in *Prometheus
Bound*. Hardy undoubtedly set out to present Napoleon

as the undisguised villain in the great tragedy of nations. This aspect of his character is the first to come to mind, and presents a direct parallel to the treatment of Xerxes in *The Persians.* Both are imperialists and militarists *par excellence,* and they go the way of all militarists in an age of budding democracy. They arouse no pity and little sympathy as their careers are unfolded, except when we get premonitory hints of the doom in store for them. At the end, however, they present truly tragic figures of fallen greatness, and commiseration is no longer withheld. Viewed in this light, Bonaparte ceases to be the pure villain and becomes, like Agamemnon, the tragic hero of the drama and the champion of his own hopeless cause against the unfeeling and resistless hand of Destiny. This impression is the one with which we are left as Napoleon makes his final appearance after Waterloo. On the other hand, instances of villainy and blackheartedness are not wanting in the poem. It is only necessary to call to mind his desertion of the remnant of the army retreating out of Russia, treated in what is perhaps the most gruesome scene in the work, and his brutal treatment of Josephine.

If Napoleon as villain and hero resembles Xerxes and Agamemnon, there is still another aspect in which he is more like the Titan Prometheus, who was gifted with foresight beyond gods and men. He often spoke of his star, and this recognition of himself as a child of Destiny makes him peculiarly fitted for a living exponent of Hardy's ideas. Both Prometheus and Bonaparte realize and advocate the claims of a higher unalterable Law against the prevailing notion of an omnipotent and be-

[247]

nevolent Personality. As Æschylus does not hesitate to declare that Zeus himself would come to grief if he disobeyed the predestined Law, so Napoleon's Promethean vision is clearly set forth in the most critical moments of his career, at the opening of the Russian campaign and at Waterloo, where he declares himself to be moved "by laws imposed on me exorably!"

Again the female characters in *The Dynasts* may be compared with the women of classical tragedy. The weak and altogether pathetic figures of the two empresses, Josephine and Marie, represent the characteristic Greek attitude towards women, as childlike, rather "no-account" people. They are in effect the only real puppets in the work, and in themselves exercise almost no influence over the main action. Essentially futile, also, is the character of Queen Louisa of Prussia. Except for his rather sentimental treatment of these women (the deathbed scene of Josephine exceeds almost anything in the novels for sheer pathos), Hardy is more typically Hellenic in his rigid subordination of female characters than is Æschylus himself. The fifty suppliant-maids, Antigone, Ismene, Atossa and perhaps also Cassandra, represent the types we expect to find in Greek tragedy and in classical literature in general, but there are no parallels in *The Dynasts* for the strength of will exhibited by Electra, and more particularly by Clytemnestra.

The supernatural plays a large rôle in most of Æschylus's tragedies and in *The Dynasts*. Both poets display a temperament taking a keen and naïve delight in playing with all the old machinery and tinsel belonging to the realm of the ghost-story. Dramatic use of prophecies,

The Cosmic Poet (1903-1908)

premonitions, ominous happenings, and similar astrological "business" is not disdained by either. There are no old-fashioned, frank, outspoken ghosts in *The Dynasts*, as there are in *The Eumenides* and *The Persians*, except for their occasional appearance in visions, such as the apparition of the Duke of Enghien to Napoleon before Waterloo. Both the "Shade of Darius" and the "Ghost of Clytemnestra" are invoked by Æschylus at opportune moments and act their parts without the scene to lose either dignity or dramatic effect. The same is not completely true of the scene in *The Dynasts* in which an enamel portrait of Marie Antoinette falls down on its face as Marie Louise of Austria consents to become Napoleon's wife. It is very dexterously explained, however, as having been caused by a natural shudder of the "Shade of the Earth" upon hearing the news. Cassandra's incoherent and blood-curdling prophecy before and during the murder of Agamemnon is paralleled by the visions and premonitions of the spirits created by Hardy. On the day of Sir John Moore's death, for instance, the Spirit of the Pities has a vision of his monument in the Garden of San Carlos.

If the excitation of the emotions of fear and pity in the audience is regarded as the ultimate aim of all tragedy, it will readily be seen how this requirement is satisfied by Hardy. At the first glance it may seem that the element of fear is stronger in Æschylus while that of pity is the dominant note in all of Hardy's work. But we must not forget the pathos of *The Suppliants*, of *Prometheus*, and of *The Persians* in our admiration for the skill with which the atmosphere of impending doom is evoked in the *Agamemnon.* Nor does the motif of terror play any minor part in *The Dynasts.* Perhaps the acme of "fear" of the usual tragic kind is reached in the presentation of the retreat of the Grand Army from Moscow through Lithuania and over the Beresina. There are not many effects that can equal the horror of the mad soldiers' song found in this section of the work. Aside from scenes of a similar nature, it will be observed that a note of terror is the ground-tone of the whole trilogy—and a deeper terror by far than any mere fear for the fate of the characters in a play could possibly inspire—a terror at the complete abandonment of the whole human race to its unknown and sinister destiny. It is a terror that strikes us all, concerns each individual personally, and all that he loves most in the world. *The Dynasts* was intended by its author not as an illusive stage-spectacle, but as a drama wherein we can see ourselves most nearly concerned. And Hardy at certain inspired moments can present it in its most ghastly aspects with overwhelming sincerity. No human feeling is quite so terrible as that of utter helplessness in the face of the unknown. But just as in reading Æschylus, one cannot emerge from the tremendous experience which a surrender of one's self to the charm of the work amounts to, without feeling that a genuine betterment and enlargement of the soul have taken place. As Mr. Abercrombie has put it:

Even more than the finest among the tragic novels, the tragic poem is full of a great pity and a great patience. It cannot comfort; but it does better. Like all great tragedy, it is "Kathartic," purging those who learn to love it of meanness and impatience and self-pity. Like all great art, it exalts and enlarges.

CHAPTER X

Janus (1925)

*I*T remains to record a few late facts.

In 1914 Hardy married his second wife, Florence Emily Dugdale, a professional writer of occasional pieces for various periodicals and newspapers and the author of a few delightful children's books. She shares the honors that have been enfolding her husband thickly in his declining years.

Upon the death of George Meredith in 1909, Hardy fell heir to the Order of Merit. He has also received an honorary Litt. D. from Cambridge, and is an Honorary Fellow of Magdalen College in that University. Aberdeen and Oxford have both made him a Doctor of Laws, the latter in spite of the not too complimentary picture of "Christminster" which figured in *Jude*. He holds the Gold Medal of the Royal Society of Literature, membership in the Council of Justice to Animals and in the Athenæum Club, and the office of Justice of the Peace for his native district. He bears these burdens very lightly, as is fitting.

For years, however, his many admirers have been raising an annual outcry—for Hardy has never been awarded the sweetest plum of all, the Nobel Prize in literature. There can, of course, be little doubt that *The Dynasts* was the most imposing and important poetic work of the first decade of our century, and may possibly be ranked ultimately with the greatest pieces in the English language. Yet the Nobel committee, having been forced to defend itself again and again for ignoring Hardy, still feels it necessary to assert its independence of outside suggestion by finding other worthy recipients of its honors. *The Queen of Cornwall,* had it been written by a younger or more obscure poet, might well have been chosen for distinction—but, no; Hardy is still just the Victorian novelist, and little better than a memory. For most people, indeed, his name would mean no more and no less if he had died thirty years ago.

For the past ten years he has been indulging in the luxury of imagining his end to be near; yet he lives on, and, what is more, manages to keep undiminished and untarnished the brightness of his poetic muse. It is still too early to say that his work is over; that was already said in 1895, in 1908, in 1914, in 1922.

* *

*

Occasionally, however, his figure is illuminated by a sudden and transitory burst of public interest. Such an occasion was afforded during the Prince of Wales's visit to Dorchester on July 19, 1923. This event was recorded as follows, by the special correspondent of the London *Times:*

The meeting of the Prince of Wales and Mr. Thomas Hardy dwarfed every other circumstance of the third and last day of the Prince's western tour. It seemed to have struck the general imagination, so much was it talked of, so thoroughly did it per-

Janus (1925)

meate to-day's programme. This was natural in Dorchester, where the position of Mr. Hardy belies the proverb about a prophet and his own country. But Dorchester was only the culmination of the meeting with Mr. Hardy.

All day long the Prince's motor-car sped through Mr. Hardy's world; not only through the very country which the great writer has transfigured for so many of us by the shifting lights of his genius, but the country he has peopled with characters that do not die like mortal men and women. Here are houses, farms, cottages, beautiful with the time-worn loveliness of Wessex; but their beauty is overlaid by their poetical interest, for in them live the spirits of Bathsheba Everdene, Gabriel Oak, Eustacia Vye, and Tess. Such habitations are familiar, though we may never have seen them before, since Mr. Hardy has the secret of giving his eyes to his readers. And with his eyes they look also at the barrows and downs that stretch along the horizon in hues of green and purple, brown and gold.

The Prince's route need not be related to Mr. Hardy's books by such links as the literary investigator loves to forge. But the veritable Hardy air is breathed forth by names like Warminster, Mere, Shaftesbury, Fordington, Poundbury Farm, Maiden Castle, and Upwey. Through some of the places they connote the Prince passed; at some he stayed to meet Duchy tenants, or for other of the various objects of his tour. Then, at last, Dorchester gave him a welcome which might have been a chapter out of an unpublished Wessex novel. That chapter would describe how a son of the Wessex soil, having lifted himself to greatness, joined in his town's greeting of a Prince, who afterwards delighted to honour him, and be honoured by him, in his own home.

The road into Dorchester cuts deeply between high, wooded banks. The banks were filled by children in simple, pretty dresses; while the road was kept by Boy Scouts and Girl Guides, who showed once or twice, when there was a mild rush, the mingled tact and determination of London policemen. A blazing sun from a quite blue sky brought out the colour wherever it

[253]

The Life of Thomas Hardy

showed among the rich green of the trees or in the heat of the beflagged and bannered road. The children's sweet, trained voices rang out in the chorus from *The Dynasts*, specially set to music:

> Now a stirring thrills the air
> Like to sounds of joyance there,
> That the rages of the ages
> Shall be cancelled,
> And deliverance offered from the darts that were;
> Consciousness the will informing
> Till it fashions all things fair.

At the top of the road the Prince was received by the Mayor and Corporation in a covered stand, where Mr. Hardy had a place. His Royal Highness was then conducted, through lines of the Dorsetshire Regiment, to a new Territorial drill-hall, which he declared open in a short speech. Those who had lived through the long years of the war, he said, would never wish to repeat the experience; but, at the same time, he was certain there was no finer training for young men than that they got in the Territorials, and he hoped the boys of Dorchester and the county would add, if need were, to the splendid record of the Dorsetshire Regiment.

Mr. Hardy was present at this ceremony. From the Drill Hall he drove with the Prince, amid the cheers of people pleased to see the young face and the old side by side, to Max Gate. As for Mr. Hardy, he may be 80-odd, but his lined countenance bore a very alert and cheerful expression, and, if it spoke truly, he enjoyed to the full the bustle and colour of the streets, and shared to the full in the joy of his fellow-townsmen.

I have already referred to the prevalent interest in the luncheon at Max Gate. It expressed itself in a desire, which in this case was wistful rather than vulgar, to overhear the conversation at that very private and informal little gathering. People spoke as though they would not have spied if they could; they only wondered what the talk of a young Prince and an aged

The Prince of Wales visits Mr. and Mrs. Hardy at Max Gate.

poet might be like. Of course, they can never know. This must be numbered among the fascinating secrets which will not be told. The house at Max Gate stands secluded among the closely growing trees that overshadow it. There was no mob at the gates. The privacy of Mr. Hardy and his guest was respected in intention no less than fact. The photograph taken after luncheon on the lawn will be the sole record of an occasion that, judging from one's experience to-day in Dorchester and on the road through Wessex, charms alike the fancy of the Hardy student and of the man who could not tell how Tess came of the D'Urbervilles.

The Prince's next visit was paid to tenants who might be said to live over the way from Mr. Hardy's. During the afternoon, still in the very region of the novels, he climbed the Maiden Castle Earthworks, sinking to the ground on the summit, declaring his pleasure at the prospect of half an hour's rest, and remaining at ease till the half-hour had gone by.

*   *

*

In all future dealings with the figure and influence of Hardy it will probably be found necessary to keep Hardy the writer and philosopher distinct from Hardy the man and personality. From reading most of his books the natural impulse is to imagine their author as a morose, grim and cynical being. This is a delusion. His surface-personality seems to be reflected only in the pure and gentle vein of humor which animates the humbler country-figures in the novels.

Hardy always regarded himself, as a writer, as a kind of æolian harp, blown upon by all the winds of the heavens, wild and gentle, good and bad, cheerful and sorrowful, sentimental and ironical, frivolous and sober. But to all this variety the harp gave but one response;

it was attuned permanently to a single chord, in a harmonious, but minor, mode. His was a nature that felt all emotions, but reacted in literature to only a few. His spirit became vocal only when stirred by tragedy. But this does not mean that he failed to perceive, understand and feel deeply the untragic amenities of existence.

In his *Hand of Ethelberta,* it is of interest to note, no less than four of the principal personages make statements which have a single bearing on the matter of the distinction to be drawn between the inner life of a writer and his imaginative works. Christopher Julian says, "People who print very warm words have sometimes very cold manners." By reversing the sense of this statement, without destroying its validity, it can be made to apply very nicely to Hardy's cold words and warm manners. Again, Ladywell says to Neigh, while discussing the common object of their admiration, "Whatever seems to be the most prominent vice, or the most prominent virtue, in anybody's writing is the one thing you are safest from in personal dealings with the writer." On the following page Neigh says substantially the same thing: "It is as risky to calculate people's ways of living from their writings as their incomes from their ways of living." The fascinating Ethelberta herself, when upbraided by Lady Petherwin for the ribaldry of her verses, defends herself as follows: "It would be difficult to show that because I have written so-called tender and gay verse, I feel tender and gay. It is too often assumed that a person's fancy is a person's real mind. I believe that in the majority of cases one is fond of imagining the direct opposite of one's principles in sheer effort after something fresh and free; at any rate, some of the lightest of those rhymes were composed between the deepest fits of dismals I have known.''

Mrs. Louise Chandler Moulton, who was very well acquainted with Hardy in the nineties, was once asked whether he was as cynical a misogynist as was implied by the pictures of the women in his *Group of Noble Dames*. She replied, ''But he doesn't think he is cynical. He thinks he is photographic. I know no man who likes women better, and there is nothing that a woman could possibly do that would seem wrong to him.'' This, it must be remembered, was the impression given by the creator of Bathsheba, whose vanity and folly, and of Arabella, whose sensuality and calculating covetousness, are the chief agents of a malignant destiny in the stories in which they enact their unenviable rôles. It was a remarkable impression, even if it be discounted by the inevitable sentimentality of its fair recorder.

Another acquaintance thus described the man in 1892: ''Mr. Hardy is in himself a gentle and singularly pleasing personality. Of middle height, with a very thoughtful face and rather melancholy eyes, he is nevertheless an interesting and amusing companion. He is regarded by the public at large as a hermit ever brooding in the far-off seclusion of a west-country village. A fond delusion, which is disproved by the fact that he is almost more frequently to be seen in a London drawing-room, or a Continental hotel, than in the quiet old-world lanes of rural Dorchester.''

One aspect of Hardy's temperament seems to have retarded somewhat a popular and universal recognition of its pleasant qualities. This is his notorious distaste for the society of the professional interviewer, the curious tourist and the idle sight-seer. Here is Samuel G. Blythe's report of an attempted interview for the *Saturday Evening Post*:

"It cannot be said, in verity, that Thomas Hardy expressed any passionate eagerness to greet me at his Wessex home, but it came about, none the less. How keenly I recall the grizzled author of *Tess* and *Jude* as he stood that morning on his terrace, and his words—the words of the master!

" 'Mr. Hardy, I have traveled three thousand miles to see you.' This reverently.

" 'Really?' This politely, but with a certain disinterestedness that was depressing.

" 'Yes, I have traveled three thousand miles to see you.' This with less reverence and more emphasis.

" 'Really?' This with an intonation that expressed, with sufficient clarity, the thought: 'Well, you've seen me; what else do you want?'

"Imagine an earnest pilgrim at a literary shrine able to dig out but two cold and clammy 'Reallys' as a starter! The situation was precarious, and needed the tonic of instant diversion into other channels.

" 'You have a lot of crows on your place.' This with an appropriate sweep of the arm that included an immense flock of black and busy birds on the lawn.

" 'My word! Those are not crows; those are rooks!' And the author of *Under the Greenwood Tree* and *Far from the Madding Crowd* proceeded along the terrace by himself—if you can picture the scene that morning with

Janus (1925)

the bright Wessex sunshine flooding the landscape—
alone, indubitably alone.''

Hardy's well-known impatience with besiegers of this
sort, although too often and too grossly exaggerated, as
above, has served to propagate the impression that he is
an incurable recluse who has foresworn the society of
his fellow-beings.

This is far from being true, however. He is not shy.
He receives casual visitors. The one common ground
upon which the personality and the works of the man
meet is that of a universal sympathy for the sufferings
of humanity, which may even, on suitable occasions, include the sufferings of journalists. This is the one
dominant Hardy-theme, and to it he long ago dedicated
both himself and his artistic work. His life and works
are one great protest against man-made and god-made
misery—against man's inhumanity to man, to woman,
and even to the lower animals.

*   *

*

Just as the figure of Thomas Hardy should be recognized as possessing the two distinct and sometimes quite
contradictory aspects of the personality and the writer,
so Hardy the writer in himself sometimes has presented
to the careful reader two quite distinct faces. The realistic and the naïve writer will frequently have to be sharply
differentiated from the philosophic and symbolic writer.
The fundamental and unconscious dilemmas and contra-
dictions underlying his later philosophy can usually be
traced back to this instinctive ability of his to divide him-

self, as it were, into quite distinct Hardys, strangers to each other.

When Hardy wrote in his intensest moods, however—whenever, that is to say, he assumed the mantle that is destined to clothe his name for posterity—he discovered his inmost relief and satisfaction to lie in the particular experience which he expressed in his motto to *The Return of the Native*:

> "To sorrow
>   I bade good morrow,
> And thought to leave her far away behind;
>   But cheerly, cheerly,
>   She loves me dearly;
> She is so constant to me, and so kind.
>   I would deceive her,
>   And so leave her,
> But ah! she is so constant and so kind."

THE END

PRINTED IN THE U. S. A. BY
THE QUINN & BODEN COMPANY
RAHWAY, N. J.